March 2024

MW01700576

Jen —

SCAFFOLDING TO THE HEART

Thank you for your encouragement, & your generous sharing of your story,

Best,

Carolina

SCAFFOLDING to the HEART

Safety-Enhancing Ideas for Narrative Trauma Work

CAROLINE J. WRIGHT

ISBN 978-1-7381084-1-1 (paperback) | ISBN 978-1-7381084-0-4 (e-book)

Cover art by Tracey Harris
Cover design by Jazmin Welch

To Michael White and the many others
who have contributed to Narrative Practice,
this book is a tribute to and celebration of your gifts.

Contents

Introduction

"WELCOME HOME." The voice of the older, distinguished-looking Hawaiian gentleman was laden with warmth; his gaze met mine with a directness and openness that was notable in its candour. I detected no agenda, no hints of expectation, no judgment one way or another in that gaze. Pure and simple, it was a wish of welcoming.

I was startled by this gift—for it did feel like a gift—and I was struck by how such a small interaction had evoked in me this sense of peace, calm, and well-being. I was the overstimulated, exhausted tourist returning back to a hotel, and this man, this sentinel of the parking lot and keeper of the gate, managed to short-circuit all the static and gift me with a profound sense of homecoming.

I remember distinctly how this exchange affected me. It quieted my mind, settled my body, and warmed my heart. I felt more comfortable and at home in my own skin. Indeed, even as I write these words now, I experience a trace of that contentment and ease.

It occurs to me why this humble exchange has stayed with me. It captures the primary purpose of my work as a therapist. It is what I strive to help others create—a feeling of peace and contentment that emanates from the very core of one's being. And it is this kind of heartfelt peace and contentment that is so often disrupted by the traumatic experience.

Hearth and Home: A Useful Metaphor for Understanding Safety

"Welcome home." It is a heartwarming phrase. It evokes images of hearth and home that are both personal and iconic. My own memories include images of family members flopped around the small living room, the fireplace ablaze with one of my father's famous fires, my teenaged self curled up with a book, my little brother quietly aligning his Matchbox cars.

My mum is marking term papers, and in the background, there is a clatter of someone in the kitchen making a cup of tea. The blizzard howls outside and the snow piles up, covering the front walkways—yet again—on this Saturday afternoon in northern Alberta. The storm accentuates the warmth of this homey scene, a scene imbued with a kind of careless intimacy.

Hearth and home—it's a seemingly timeless and familiar phrase depicted in art and literature through the ages. A quick internet search of images produces a plethora of scenes from ancient times to modern day. The hearth is the focal point of the home, the source of both food and warmth, providing sustenance for the body.

From the medieval images of grand hallways with rows of tables flanking a massive masonry hearth and a roast boar cooking on the spit to the modern-day house party where everyone seems to gravitate towards the kitchen, the hearth is a place of welcoming and connection. It is not a surprise to me that the hearth becomes the gathering place, for it is so often the relational place, the place where we not only feed our bellies but also our hearts, minds, and souls. It is a place designed for nurturing all aspects of ourselves. And as such, it is a quintessential symbol of safety.

But what if someone's particular experience of hearth and home has been damaged by the heart-wrenching and soul-destroying impacts of trauma? What then? It can change everything and make almost every aspect of venturing out into the world a fearsome challenge.

I find this concept of hearth and home to be a useful metaphor for understanding how to create safety for individuals as they reclaim those precious and dear aspects of their lives that have been impacted by trauma. As the hearth represents the centre of the home, so does the heart represent those central, most-cherished aspects of oneself.

Leaning heavily on Developmental Psychology and Narrative Practice, and placing an emphasis on safety, I have enlisted a home-building analogy—hearth and home being the central metaphor—as a means for sharing practice ideas. These ideas are aimed at assisting individuals to be the architects of their own recovery.

The History of This Book

The ideas for this work germinated from the ashes of my despair right around the time I was wrapping up the research for my master's thesis on child sexual abuse. I had begun my degree with a clear vision of gathering more training and knowledge to be better prepared to assist children and their families who have experienced tremendous hardship.

This desire to be of service to children and families developed during the preceding three years when I worked as a child and youth counsellor in an intensive care residential treatment home. In this role, I worked with children and youth who had experienced all kinds of hardship—physical, emotional, and sexual abuse as well as neglect and severe physical and mental challenges.

During this time, I was regularly struck by the resiliency and tenacity of these young people. They inspired me to figure out better ways to be an instrument of hope and caring for others who are going through tough times.

This led me to an educational psychology master's program with a clinical psychology specialization. This degree married my interest in children's development and learning with my desire to assist individuals who were struggling with serious (i.e., "clinical") concerns.

During the practicum portion of my degree, I had the opportunity to train and conduct research in a family therapy program that dealt with child sexual abuse. This placement perfectly matched my aspirations. It was the early 1990s, and these kinds of treatment programs were relatively new to the world of mental health, at least in my Canadian part of the world.

I was in my mid-20s, keen and energized, and itching to embark on my career as a clinician. I was ready to join the fray and do my bit in helping children and their families become healthier and happier people—so ready, that is, until the day that I had The Realization. At the conclusion of my clinical practicum, I was confronted with what was to me an alarming discovery: I could not do this particular type of work.

As a student, I had experienced the therapy sessions as heavy, oppressive, and overwhelming, laden with feelings of despair, helplessness, and shame. In particular, my memory of those sessions included vivid images of the children's faces; they looked so stricken. I could not see myself conducting sessions such as these with the kind of calm and caring proficiency demonstrated by my clinical supervisor. That is, I recognized that I did not believe myself capable of managing the kind of intense feelings of devastation that I would encounter in this type of work.

Furthermore, I believed that if I could not confidently manage the intensity of those sessions as a practitioner, then I certainly was not in any position to assist those who would seek counselling from me.

The Realization was this: With respect to the work about which I was so passionate, I could not conceive of how to do it in such a way that I could be sure I was facilitating healing rather than furthering harm. I could not hold a place of hope, strength, and, most importantly, safety.

I was halted in my therapeutic tracks. It was clear to me that I was in over my head. I did not have the skills, knowledge, confidence, or whatever combination of tools was necessary to do this work without the risk of causing harm.

Reflecting back, I believe that along with this realization was born the fear of being an agent of re-traumatization. And in response to this fear, I developed a preoccupation with creating greater safety in the therapy session.

I am not alone in this. A concern about safety and re-traumatization is a common one for practitioners. I believe it is what has sparked so many new and innovative practices. This safety concern is the primary driver behind my desire to share the ideas in this book.

Thanks to Narrative Therapy, I did find a way back to working from a place of hope and safety with children and youth who were experiencing hardship. However, to do so, I distanced myself from the more intense territory of working *directly* with the original trauma experience. Instead, I focused on working with what I saw as the fallout or the effects of the trauma experience—problems of life such as addictions, family and school troubles, and mental health challenges.

At the same time, I continued to search for the missing pieces in my repertoire that would give me the assurance I needed to work more directly and safely with trauma. This book presents those safety pieces that I've found have the most impact on enhancing safety for narrative trauma work.

The Central Influences for This Book

CLINICAL AND DEVELOPMENTAL PSYCHOLOGY

In completing countless psycho-educational, social-emotional, and risk assessments while working with children and youth in educational and clinical treatment settings, I developed an appreciation for the vast range and complexity of ways that individuals learn and make meaning for themselves in their lives.

Lev Vygotsky's developmental theory of cognitive processing became a central organizing principle around which I developed ways to work with young children and youth. Of particular relevance for me is Vygotsky's concept of the zone of proximal development (ZPD) in which he described a child's learning process:

> The zone of proximal development … is the distance between the actual developmental level as determined by independent problem solving and the level of potential development as determined through problem solving under adult guidance or collaboration with more capable peers.[1]

The ZPD speaks to a person's readiness to learn; it refers to the level of understanding a person experiences when they are unable to master the next level of learning *independently* but can readily do so *with support or guidance* from another person. To me, the ZPD is the cutting edge of learning. It is the place of potential or of possibility, cognitively speaking. It is the place of learning and development where the unknown becomes known.

The idea is that a more knowledgeable other—whether that person be a sophisticated peer, a teacher, a parent, or a therapist—provides just enough support such that an individual is able to move to a higher level of learning or to a new pertinent way of making meaning. This support or guidance has been described as scaffolding in the developmental literature.[2]

Just as a steel scaffold aids workers in constructing a building, so also does a conceptual scaffold aid learners in constructing new meanings. I have found the concepts of the ZPD and of scaffolding to be guiding principles to hold close when working with people across a wide range of problems.

---

1 Vygotsky, L. S. (1978). *Mind in society: The development of higher psychological processes*. Harvard University Press. p. 86.

2 Wood, D., Bruner, J., & Ross, G. (1976). The role of tutoring in problem solving. *The Journal of Child Psychology and Psychiatry, 17*, pp. 89–100.

NARRATIVE PRACTICE

When I first heard Michael White's ideas, I remember experiencing a strong sense of coming home. At the time, I was working as a clinician in a treatment foster care program. His ideas had (and still have) an enormous resonance for me.

Since that day, I have continued to feel inspired and exhilarated by his work and that of several other narrative practitioners. David Epston, Maggie Carey, David Denborough, Cheryl White, Shona Russell, Alice Morgan, and Angel Yuen are just a few of the narrative practitioners whose ideas have had a major impact on my thinking and practice. Just seeing their names in print sends a frisson of excitement through me that stems from the knowledge that they are such a rich source of ideas for change, possibility, and hope.

The learning I received from the Narrative Therapy community helped me to foster the kind of therapeutic stance that I believe is requisite for trauma work. Key narrative ideas and practices for this work include the de-centred but influential relationship, re-authoring and externalizing conversations, the concept of the absent but implicit, and the use of metaphor and therapeutic documentation.

These ideas and practices are geared towards supporting the development of the individual's greater sense of personal agency or power over the problem experience. They accomplish this by making explicit, and then carefully considering, the relations of power operating in the individual's life context.

Narrative Therapy gave me hopeful and compassionate ways of working with children, youth, and their parents in treatment and system contexts (e.g., school, hospital, and legal). In these mostly professional-centred, and often pathology-focused settings, I strived to foster the individual's preferred story. For example, as a counsellor in youth outreach programs, externalizing and re-authoring conversations gave me the means to explore with youth how they could stand in their value of self-determination given the constraints of the various systems impacting their lives.

At a treatment foster-care program, I relished the task assigned by my supervisor to revise the clinical intake forms to reflect a greater focus on wellness rather than pathology. The result was a form, while still documenting critical incidents and concerns, focused primarily on the youth's skills, knowledges, commitments, and hopes. This process led me to develop intake interviews that matched this wellness focus.

In the school system, I saw my diagnostic assessment reports as therapeutic documents that mapped the effects of the problem. In addition to sharing test results and their implications, I made sure to include the student's and parents' commitments, hopes, skills, and knowledges and any sparkling moments of resilience that I had noticed in our assessment interviews. The meeting to share test results with the student and parents became an opportunity to renegotiate their idea of the problem and to begin re-authoring their preferred story in relation to the problem.

A suicide and self-harm risk assessment was no longer just about finding out how safe a youth felt from self-harm. It also became an opportunity for externalizing and re-authoring conversations about problems of life like sadness, hopelessness, and overwhelm and about discovering ways to stand up to those problems.

When White incorporated Vygotsky's ideas and the concept of scaffolding into his work,[3] I experienced a second kind of homecoming with regard to Narrative Practice. Applying these ideas to my narrative therapy practice, I used my knowledge of methods of inquiry as a kind of scaffold, which provides enough support for the individual to construct their[4] own new preferred meanings and understandings about the trauma experience.

I see a scaffold as being any kind of therapeutic structure that facilitates this desired change process. As well, it can be viewed in particular or in broad terms. In particular terms, I see scaffolding as including specific practices such as the use of metaphors, therapeutic documentation, editorializing techniques, breath work techniques, check-ins, and so on.

In broad terms, I view all narrative practices as providing a kind of scaffold for the individual, and this includes the establishment of the de-centred but influential therapeutic relationship as well as externalizing and re-authoring conversations. All of these practices lend structure to therapeutic conversations that assist individuals in uncovering their preferred alternative story.

SOLUTION-FOCUSED BRIEF THERAPY

This therapy modality, including single-session work in particular,[5] showed me that important positive change, even for problems

3 White, M. (2007). *Maps of Narrative Practice*. W. W. Norton & Company.

4 Out of respect for diverse gender identities, this book uses "they" and its other forms to refer to singular indefinite nouns, even though it is grammatically atypical to do so.

5 The practitioners at Eastside Family Centre in Calgary, Canada, showed me the beauty of single session work. See Harper-Jaques, S., McElheran, N., Slive, A., & Leahey, M. (2009). A comparison of two approaches to the delivery of walk-in single session mental health therapy. *Journal of Systemic Therapies, 27*(4), pp. 44–53.

with a long and complicated history, can occur in a relatively short time. I often witnessed this kind of timely relief inspire a new sense of hope for people. I learned about how this sense of hope aids in alleviating the heavy despair that so often accompanies trauma work and can stall the healing process.

As well, time constraints taught me to better gear therapy towards what makes the most sense for the individual at that particular moment in time. It led me to discover that effective and timely intervention is often very meaningful intervention.

The work of Steve de Shazer,[6] Insoo Kim Berg,[7] and Scott Miller[8] has had a major influence on my thinking. From this body of work, I welcomed into my narrative practice strategies such as scaling questions and various renditions of the miracle question. These proved to be useful tools for me as I endeavoured to provide the "good fit" scaffold that would support individuals in re-authoring their preferred story.

MIND-BODY-BRAIN SCIENCES

The work of people such as Bessel van der Kolk,[9] Gabor Maté,[10] and Daniel Siegel[11] gave me a richer understanding of the physiological side of meaning-making in relation to traumatic events. Some of

---

6 de Shazer, S. (1985). *Keys to solution in brief therapy*. W. W. Norton & Company.

7 De Jong, P., & Berg, I. K. (1998). *Interviewing for solutions*. Thomson Brooks/Cole Publishing Co.

8 Prescott, D. S., Maeschalck, C. L., & Miller, S. D. (Eds.). (2017). *Feedback-informed treatment in clinical practice: Reaching for excellence* (1st ed.). American Psychological Association.

9 van der Kolk, B. A. (2015). *The body keeps score: Brain, mind, and body in the healing of trauma*. Penguin Books.

10 Maté, G. (2010). *In the realm of hungry ghosts: Close encounters with addiction*. North Atlantic Books.

11 Siegel, D. (2012). *Pocket guide to interpersonal neurobiology: An integrative handbook of the mind*. W. W. Norton & Company.

the key understandings I gathered from this body of work include the complexity of how the body encodes trauma, the need for integration of different kinds of information—including emotional, cognitive, and physiological—and the concept of neuroplasticity, that is, the brain's ability to change its structure in response to experience.

It was my exploration into this work that prompted me to privilege the "voice" of the body in a more intentional and methodical manner as it pertains to safety when healing from the effects of trauma.

BODY-MIND PRACTICES

Meditation and yoga as well as other mindfulness practices[12] have expanded my understanding regarding the possibilities of how to integrate various kinds of information. In particular, learning about breathing techniques and body scans used in these disciplines offered me some practical tools that help an individual integrate new meanings and understandings developed within the therapeutic conversation.

I came to see mindfulness meditation and centring practices as having great value, not only for those with whom I worked but also for me. Utilizing these kinds of techniques supports the individual to be in charge of the therapy process, and in particular, they assist the individual to keep the therapy in a safe place. Maintaining my own meditation and grounding practices helps me to sustain a calm, grounded presence in sessions, a stance that

12 Kabat-Zinn, J. (2009). *Full catastrophe living: Using the wisdom of your body and mind to face stress, pain and illness*. Bantam Dell.

I believe contributes to creating a safe therapeutic space. These practices have become an integral part of the way I work.

It was this last small but important piece—the body-mind practice piece—that completed the trauma therapy puzzle for me. Including body awareness and breath work techniques into the therapeutic conversation gave me the assurance I needed that the work could unfold in a safe manner. With this last piece in place, I felt more confident that I could work safely alongside individuals and, metaphorically speaking, assist them to create their own sense of hearth and home.

The Structure of This Book

In using the metaphor of restoring or reconstructing the hearth and home to illustrate ideas for creating safety in trauma work, I have drawn up some possible sets of "house plans." These combine Narrative Therapy practices with safety tools for the purpose of assisting the individual in designing and building (or rebuilding) the sanctuary for the self. Whether it be constructing a foundation of a safe therapeutic relationship or doing the restoration work with core truths, these practices aim to support individuals in constructing their own hearth and home and, in so doing, finding a heartfelt sense of peace and contentment.

Though I see this work as having a clear developmental progression—that is, each stage or set of therapeutic tasks builds upon the next—it is not linear. However, I outline the main ideas in a linear manner for clarity of explanation.

In a nutshell, the four main sets of practices that anchor my therapeutic process for safely navigating trauma work are:

1. **CHAPTER 1: LAYING THE FOUNDATION** of safety with the individual regarding the therapeutic process primarily through careful cultivation of a de-centred but influential therapeutic relationship
2. **CHAPTERS 2 AND 3: DEVELOPING SAFETY TOOLS** through the provision of a range of practices that assist the individual *and* the practitioner in holding and sustaining a place of safety during the session. These include restorative and constructive breath work practices, safety check-ins, therapy worries work, and other body-mind strategies.
3. **CHAPTER 4: FRAMING UP THE STRUCTURE** through the deconstruction and reconstruction work of externalizing and re-authoring conversations, which is central to creating a structure strong and stable enough to support the core trauma work that is to follow
4. **CHAPTERS 5 AND 6: RESTORING THE HEARTH** by relying heavily on the concept of the absent but implicit, which is central for structuring the re-authoring conversations that occur during what I refer to as the core trauma work. The central absent-but-implicit question during this stage of the therapeutic process is: What was it that is precious and dear to you, was violated by the trauma (or hardship) experience?

Three individuals with whom I have worked—Julia, Grace, and Cory—stepped up to aid me in bringing my therapeutic process to life by offering me their stories of transformation. All three continued to be involved in the writing of this book by reviewing the sections that pertained to them and offering feedback and revisions to their story.

For purposes of clarity, I have also included other individuals' experiences (e.g., Cheyenne) or composites of several individuals (e.g., Josie) to better illustrate some of the practice ideas. This is the case in Chapters 1 through 3 where I describe the foundational safety practices of the de-centred but influential relationship, the breath work techniques, and the safety check-ins, and practitioner self-care. In order to protect the privacy of all the individuals who so generously gifted their experiences to this book, I have modified several aspects of their stories, including identifying information.

In Chapter 4, Julia, Grace, and Cory's stories allow me to illustrate the application of the narrative therapeutic practices of externalizing and re-authoring conversations integrated with the safety practices. Chapter 5 is mostly autobiographical and describes my own encounter with a hardship experience and how it informed my practice.

This leads into the practice examples of the core trauma work in Chapter 6 where we rejoin Julia, Grace, and Cory as they continue their journey of reclaiming their lives from the traumatic experiences.

The Intent of This Book

This book is about safety. Through the telling of my practitioner story, I seek to offer some ideas for enhancing safety in Narrative Practice. It is a collection of those trauma-sensitive practice pieces that I have found helpful for sustaining a safe therapeutic process.

More importantly, these are the practice pieces that the individuals with whom I have worked have found helpful. In essence, it is a summary of my efforts to apply the brilliant ideas from different disciplines and arrange them into a structure of therapeutic practices that are geared towards securing safety for the individual.

My preoccupation with safety combined with my developmental psychology lens required that I address the entire therapeutic process. It did not feel safe to me to talk about just one part of the process. I see each stage of the therapy journey as building on the next stage; there is a developmental progression of Narrative Therapy practices and an accompanying progression of safety practices.

And so, my intention here is to describe the therapy process from that moment of first contact with an individual to that last moment in the final therapy session when the individual decides that they have arrived at their healing destination.

This book is based on the acknowledgement that though this kind of work is typically extremely hard work, it need not be hopeless and despairing work. In my experience, healing from the effects of trauma can occur in releasing, liberating, and sometimes even joyful ways. It can happen without re-traumatization, and given certain contexts, it can happen relatively quickly.

In other words, this book is about sharing ideas on how to support individuals to return home to themselves. Home is that place where they are not only able to protect and nurture those aspects of themselves that are so very precious and dear but also can stand up to ongoing trials, tribulations, worries, concerns, doubts, and fears, or whatever else the world throws at them. It is a place where they can live in accordance with their preferences, values, hopes, dreams, and intentions; it is a place of sustenance and sanctuary.

CHAPTER 1

Laying the Foundation: The De-centred but Influential Relationship

I SLOWLY MADE MY WAY out of the crowded lecture theatre, wedged in on all sides by 200 other avid counsellor types; we shuffled and bumped our way through the doors. I do not do well in crowded spaces. I was painfully aware of the press of overheated bodies as I made my way through the crowd.

I drifted into the relatively open area of the foyer, searching for a friendly face and a place to anchor myself in this sea of humanity for the duration of the break. No luck. I clutched my bike helmet to my chest and did my best to avoid taking anyone out with my backpack. I scanned the crowd, seeking the easiest path through the eddies of people that were forming and re-forming around me.

As I looked up, I locked eyes with an older gentleman. This was not just any older gentleman; he was the presenter I'd come to see at this workshop. He was somewhat of a celebrity to me. I tried not to engage in hero worship (tricky, as I think his ideas are absolutely brilliant) because I had just seen him explicitly and respectfully decline the mantle of expert that the lecture host tried to bestow on him.

It was this sage of the therapy world who had caught my eye, and much to my alarm, he was directing a question at me. I was going to have to form a sentence; I was on the verge of being completely overcome. This was heightened by the knowledge that I was doubtful I could hide the fact that I was completely in awe, starstruck, dumbfounded (literally) by his mere presence.

The buzz of the crowd combined with the raucous chaos of my inner thoughts made it difficult for me to hear what he said, let alone process it. He repeated himself. "So, you biked here?" He pointed to my helmet.

What transpired next was an animated and surprisingly easy conversation about our shared passion for all things cycling. The ga-ga factor that was threatening to envelope me evaporated almost instantly, and I soon found myself chatting away with a fellow avid cyclist, not the celebrated master therapist. My original conception of this learned man—the guru, the luminary, the brilliant theoretician and master practitioner—became irrelevant and dropped out of the picture. It was classic Michael White.

The De-centred but Influential Relationship

This particular conversation occurred circa 1995, yet it resonates with me still. In a mere snippet of time, Michael White had managed to create a connection with me that sidestepped the mundane platitudes so common in similar types of impersonal social encounters.

He also invited me to step away from the expert-novice dynamic that is likely (and expected) in this context. He put me at ease, or perhaps it is more accurate to say he provided the structure that allowed me to find my ease. It gave me a peek into what it might be like to be on the receiving end of a de-centred conversation.

By being genuinely curious and interested—asking me things in such a manner that it was apparent what I had to say was of value—he created the context that allowed me to join the conversation with confidence and ease. And this happened despite my overly excited state. I forgot that I was freaking out about the possibility of disrespecting him with my misplaced admiration.

Though brief, this experience has continued to inform my practice. It acts as a mini model for developing the kind of de-centred but influential relationship that I strive to create in the therapeutic context.

For me, the pertinent features of this conversation are that it was safe, respectful, and reciprocal. What contributed to making it feel this way was, first, the almost palpable curiosity about my opinions and ideas; second, the genuine interest in what I was talking about; and last but not least, the absence of any assumptions or conclusions about what I had to say. I felt that what I had to offer was indeed privileged information.

I believe that Michael White was demonstrating some of the key elements of the de-centred but influential position. And I believe it is this kind of connection with a person that allows them the time and space for self-reflection as well as the opportunity to unpack, sort, and reconstruct problems. It leads to the kind of relationship that makes the individual feel comfortable enough to take risks and explore more possibilities.

Such is the context I aim to create in therapy sessions. As Michael White describes, it is a relationship where the therapist's stance is a de-centred one "in that the therapist is not the author of people's positions on the problems and predicaments of their lives."[13] However, he also describes it as an influential one where, through the structuring of particular practices or methods of inquiry (e.g., externalization, re-authoring), people recognize and develop those knowledges, skills, beliefs, commitments, and desires that reduce the influence of problems.

This positioning, together with what Michael White calls "editorializing" (i.e., reflective listening, open-ended questions, clarifying, and summarizing),[14] forms the basis for de-centred but influential conversations. Narrative Practice's emphasis on relationship, the de-centred but influential stance in particular, is very much in keeping with the consensus that a key variable for determining the efficacy of therapy is the nature of the therapeutic alliance.

Once established, the de-centred but influential position provides a platform for narrative practices, whether mapping the effects during externalizing conversations or exploring commitments and values in re-authoring conversations. These kinds of therapeutic conversations facilitate a shift from the person's negative identity conclusions grounded in problem-saturated stories to more positive and preferred identity conclusions derived from previously neglected stories. The result is the development of a preferred story, one which privileges the individual's beliefs, values, wishes, commitments, and conclusions about their lived experience.

At the heart of the work is the de-centred but influential relationship. This is because the de-centred but influential relationship works towards creating a safe context in which the

---

13 White, M. (2007). *Maps of narrative practice*. W. W. Norton & Company. p. 39.
14 White, M. (2007). *Maps of narrative practice*. W. W. Norton & Company. p. 45.

person can learn to be in the driver's seat of their own change process. It involves therapeutic conversations that allow the person to navigate away from a place of threat or danger, hopelessness, helplessness, overwhelm, and despair towards one of safety, confidence, hope, and possibility.

In other words, this work involves a renegotiation of the individual's relationship with the problems of life (i.e., the effects of trauma) from one of being pushed around or defined by the problems to one of being in charge of the problems in ways that fit with the person's preferred sense of identity.

Accordingly, the de-centred but influential relationship inherently creates safety. However, I have found that working with trauma in certain contexts requires additional safeguards. In particular, I am referring to those situations in which an individual is seeking therapy for a traumatic experience, and in doing this work, they encounter an intense emotional component that feels not only unsettling but also unsafe.

My intention is to offer some ideas about how the de-centred but influential relationship can be sustained and bolstered in the face of the intense challenges that are particular to working with trauma. The remainder of this chapter explores those ideas.

The De-centred but Influential Relationship in Trauma Therapy

Creating and sustaining the de-centred but influential position can be tricky at the best of times. For me, navigating this position in the context of trauma work is especially challenging. The reason for this is the danger factor. The trauma experience expropriates an individual's sense of personal agency, often leaving the person feeling vulnerable, violated, and powerless.

Consequently, as individuals approach the task of addressing the effects of trauma in therapy, they may become overwhelmed with feelings of despair and terror. They are "in danger" of losing themselves to these powerful and all-encompassing emotions. Therapy can become too scary, too hard, and too distressing.

I have come to the conclusion that creating safety by managing the dysregulation resulting from this sense of danger is key to effective, sustainable, and non-traumatizing work. However, I struggle with the fact that the very practices that help to create safety can also jeopardize the integrity of the de-centred but influential relationship.

That is, in order for the danger to be managed and enough safety created, I need to take more responsibility and provide the necessary safety measures. This is especially true at the onset of the work when the individual is experiencing more distress and uncertainty.

In other words, in the name of safety, I need to step into a more centred position where my ideas about safety are privileged over the individual's. But my intention is that this privileging of therapist ideas is both temporary and limited in scope.

As the individual becomes adept at self-regulating overwhelming emotions, the therapist can relinquish responsibility around safety and return to a more de-centred position. Nonetheless, it is a deviation from the more de-centred but influential position that is intended to be the mainstay throughout the majority of the trauma work.

While I find that stepping into a more centred position is necessary for creating enough safety, I try to do so in such a way that I remain wary of this stance. In relation to issues of safety and, in fact, throughout the therapeutic process, it is important for me to be mindful about how easily the practitioner can step too firmly into a position of authority.

One defining element of the traumatic experience is the individual's sense of a complete loss of personal power and control. Because of this, I am concerned about moving too strongly into a position of authority and inadvertently recreating a context reminiscent of previous traumatic experiences. This runs the risk of interfering with the individual's ability to access their sense of personal agency, which would detract from their ability to stand up to and manage the effects of trauma. I worry that it could lead to the person feeling re-traumatized.

Practices for Managing the De-centred but Influential Relationship When Addressing Safety

I see it as imperative to remain vigilant in order to monitor and maintain the balance of solidly holding a safe therapeutic space while simultaneously allowing the individual to reclaim as much power and control as is safely manageable. I strive for this balance by:

1. At the onset of therapy, ensuring that what I have to offer is a good fit for the individual. I do this by providing clear

expectations regarding the therapeutic process and conveying how I can be of service. The pre-therapy map and first-session therapy map discussed in this chapter are key to this process.

2 Privileging my knowledge/expertise only in the arena of danger/safety management; this is most relevant when introducing the specific safety tools described in Chapter 2 and at certain times during the core trauma work described in Chapters 5 and 6.

3 Over the course of therapy, working to shift this privileging of expertise (i.e., that of danger/safety management) and responsibility over to the individual when it is safe to do so. This means responding to the individual's increasing proficiency and confidence in managing their own sense of safety by moving to a more supporting role rather than a directing role. (This is discussed further in Chapter 2.)

4 Throughout the course of therapy, using a collaborative and consultative teaching approach rather than a directive and prescriptive teaching approach when I do step into a more centred position (for example, when introducing the body-mind techniques as detailed in Chapter 2).

5 Over the course of therapy, checking in frequently with the individual by asking them if what I'm saying makes sense. This is a common narrative practice used at all stages of the work.

6 Throughout the course of therapy, utilizing self-monitoring strategies (e.g., the Sound Check described in this chapter).

To help manage these tasks, I have created a few practice pieces that allow me to move more easily along the de-centred continuum. I wish to outline three of the most helpful ones here:

- the pre-therapy map
- the first-session therapy map
- the Sound Check

INTRODUCTORY THERAPY MAPS

A major challenge to remaining de-centred enough lies in the very nature of the practitioner role itself. Michael White acknowledges this therapist vulnerability and goes on to observe how difficult it is to achieve a de-centred but influential position.[15] This is because the people with whom practitioners meet are invariably experiencing all kinds of distress and are desperate to alleviate that distress. Consequently, it is tempting to respond by offering all kinds of advice and expert counsel, thereby positioning oneself squarely in the centre.

At times, I have felt that individuals are not just inviting me to step into the advice-giving position but *imploring* me to do so. "Tell me what to do!" is often the message my oh-so-compassionate therapist ears hear as individuals recount their concerns.

Also, some individuals with whom I have worked have expressed a certain weariness towards counsellors who respond to a concern with either a question of their own or a reflection paraphrasing the concern. These individuals have come to

---

15 White, M. (2007). *Maps of narrative practice*. W. W. Norton & Company. p. 39.

therapy with the idea of receiving the knowledge and expertise of the therapist in the form of direct advice and prescriptive information.

In response to these types of invitations, I have developed a protocol for myself that includes what I call introductory therapy maps: a pre-therapy map and a first-session therapy map. Both types of therapy maps serve the function of introducing the de-centred but influential stance.

The first-session therapy map builds upon the pre-therapy map, but both work together to create a safe therapeutic alliance that supports individuals to be more in charge of their own change process. The purpose of the maps is to clarify therapy expectations, both for myself and for the individual with whom I am working.

By "clarifying expectations," I mean clearly articulating how I practice. This includes describing my therapeutic approach and, in particular, the de-centred but influential way in which I endeavour to work. It is a useful screening process that allows individuals who prefer a different approach to choose to work with a different therapist instead.

Being explicit about what I can offer allows the individual to have a clearer idea about what therapy with me would look like. It reduces feelings of uncertainty, and it also allows individuals to make a judgment about whether or not this type of work is a fit for them. This fosters personal agency, which contributes to a sense of safety.

The Pre-therapy Map

I offer individuals who are seeking my services a 15-to-30-minute pre-therapy consultation via telephone. It is during this conversation that I map out the therapeutic process. I also explain how I work so we can determine if we are a good fit to work together.

Following is a sample script of this type of telephone conversation:

> *Hi, Grace. I want to give you an idea of how I work. So, I understand from your email that you are interested in some counselling to help you deal with some past abuse.* [I would use the individual's words verbatim here.] *This phone call is to figure out if you and I are a good fit, to see if you think that we could work well together on your concerns.*
>
> *Because you have already outlined to me in your message some of the things you wish to work on, I was thinking it would make sense for me to take some time now to provide you with some information about how I would work in relation to those concerns. Is that okay with you?*
>
> [The individual verbally agrees.]
>
> *My background is working with individuals who have experienced hardship and trauma. Primarily, I work from a narrative approach, which is a collaborative, strength-based way of working. The collaborative part means that I am very interested in receiving feedback and impressions from you as we work about how the work is going. It's important for me to*

hear from you when things don't make sense or are not heading in the right direction for you. That way, I can shift what I'm doing to better match your priorities.

I believe that when people seek out my help, it is because the problems of life have gained unwanted influence over them, and these problems have led them in a direction that they didn't want or intend. Therapy is about addressing these problems in such a way that the person is able to reclaim what is important to them and take their life in the direction they desire.

One thing that is important for you to know is that I believe feeling safe while you do this work is a top priority. Because abuse and trauma memories often are accompanied by the distressing emotions a person experienced at the time—fear and anguish, for example—I will not be asking you to explicitly re-tell any past incidents of abuse. In the way that I work, that is not a requirement for healing from the effects of the abuse. Rather, we will focus on identifying the effects, developing ways of standing up to or managing those effects, and strengthening any values and commitments that have been thwarted by those effects.

Another important thing for you to know is that because there is often a strong physiological, or body, component to the effects of abuse, I also incorporate body-mind techniques into the conversation to address those aspects. Most often, that looks like a type of breath work that I will show you in the first session. This helps to keep our work in a place that feels safe.

Does this make sense to you? Do you have any questions about what I've said?

The First-Session Therapy Map

The first-session therapy map outlines the entire therapeutic process; it is an overall plan of the service I am able to offer to the individual. Its purpose and intent is identical to the pre-therapy consultation. The difference is the pre-therapy map is usually a briefer overview of how I work and is purely a sharing of information.

In contrast, the first-session therapy map has a stronger focus on the safety aspects of the work. As well, it is more of a conversation rather than a direct sharing of information; it includes questions that focus on the individual's specific concerns, wishes, and desires for the work.

Below is a possible script of a first-session therapy map conversation. I have highlighted three parts of the conversation. The first focuses on how I work, the second on the particular safety issue of direct re-tellings, and the third on the importance of safety in general.

If I have not already explained my narrative practice approach in a pre-therapy conversation, then I would include that description in the first part of this conversation.

PART 1: AFFIRMING THE DE-CENTRED BUT INFLUENTIAL APPROACH

First, I seek to develop the de-centred but influential relationship by introducing a checking-in process. I also introduce the narrative practice of externalizing the problem. To illustrate, here is a sample script:

> *So, to start off, I would like to just spend some time describing how I work and what our work together could look like. Does that sound okay to you?*
>
> [The individual verbally agrees.]
>
> *Alright. Please feel free to interrupt me and ask me any questions you may have.*
>
> *I see it as my job to support and facilitate what you want. In this case, you have written that you wish "to heal from abuse and change family dynamics."* [I quote directly from the person's intake form.]
>
> *With regards to healing from abuse, I see it as my job to help you identify the effects of the abuse on your life, find out some of the ways you have already stood up to these effects so far, and to help you develop more or better ways of managing those effects that are still causing trouble for you. Part of our work could be finding out what your life would be like if you were "to heal from abuse," and looking into the kind of "family dynamics" you are interested in promoting in your life and what might be the steps you could take to create these family dynamics.*
>
> *Does that make sense?* [I tend to rush things a bit, so I need to remind myself to pause longer, take more time to wait for a response, and loiter a bit more. In addition to checking in

with the individual, asking "Does that make sense?" helps me do this.]

It is helpful for me if you let me know when I say something that doesn't fit for you, doesn't make sense, or is just dead wrong as far as you are concerned. Are you okay with doing that?

[The individual verbally agrees.]

Great. Your feedback helps me to stay on the right track and to figure out how best to support you. In fact, I will feel relieved when I hear you say things like "No, that isn't it. That's not what I meant." I use your feedback as guideposts that tell me if I am heading in a direction that works for you or if I have veered off course.

PART 2: ADDRESSING THE IDEA OF RE-TELLINGS

Next, I speak to the "how" and "why" of direct re-tellings as this is a key safety piece. Direct re-tellings of traumatic events can be helpful in healing, but I have found they are not *required* for healing.

As well, in the early stages of the work, I believe that re-tellings have a higher likelihood of leading to re-traumatization. Conversely, I have observed that re-tellings of the event *after* the important transformative trauma work has been completed can be very potent in the healing process. It is the timing and context of the re-telling that is key.

If it happens too early and before certain work has been completed, it runs the risk of feeding the adverse effects and inadvertently strengthening the hardship story. If it happens later, it can enhance and strengthen the preferred story. This is a key understanding that is most relevant to the core trauma work, which I explore further in Chapters 5 and 6.

For now, here is an example of how I address this safety piece in the first session:

> *Okay, so that is a general overview of how I work. Now I want to mention an important aspect about the way I work with regard to childhood abuse.* [The problem word here is the one that the individual brings to the conversation or one that they have agreed fits for how they would describe it.]
>
> *I will not ask nor expect you to provide me with any explicit details or direct re-tellings of the distressing experience(s). However, if you wish to do that, that is okay, but I will not ask or expect you to do that.*
>
> *Also, I don't see the detailed recounting of your experience of abuse as a requirement for moving on from the effects of that abuse. My reason for this approach is to avoid the risk that direct re-tellings could lead to strengthening the negative effects of the abuse (i.e., re-traumatization).* [If the individual has brought up the word re-traumatization, then I may use it here. Otherwise, I avoid it because it is one of those clinical words that has been historically associated with the privileging of therapist knowledge.] *Though this is certainly not always the case, I don't want to risk it.*
>
> *I have learned from working with others that in order to heal from the abuse, one does not have to go into "the pit of despair"*

> *(or whatever you would call that experience when you are under the influence of the negative effects) by reliving the incident in the form of a detailed re-telling. It is an option, but one I am cautious of starting with.*
>
> *Instead, I work from the premise that though this work can be very hard, sometimes exhausting and challenging work, it doesn't have to be overwhelming, hopeless, and despairing work. This hard work can stay in the realm of hope and safety. It does not have to traverse into the territory of horror and despair in order for healing to occur. We do this by keeping our work in a safe place, and in the beginning, direct re-tellings often do not feel like safe work.*
>
> *To keep our work safe, we will focus on the effects of the experience and how to manage those effects, and uncovering the commitments and values that have been impacted by those effects. We will also look at the types of commitments and values that were subjugated or violated by the abuse experience itself and explore how you can re-integrate them more fully back into your life.* [By addressing direct re-tellings in this way, I have also introduced the narrative practices of externalization and the idea of the absent but implicit that is key for the core trauma work (Chapters 4–6).]

When I have spoken with individuals as they've reflected back on their healing journey, they have identified that not being required to re-tell the particulars of the traumatizing experience was key in helping them do the work effectively. Because of this feedback, I ensure that this aspect is addressed in the first session regardless of whether I have already mentioned it during a pre-therapy conversation. For me, the importance of this understanding to the therapeutic process is such that it bears repetition.

PART 3: MAKING EXPLICIT THE IMPORTANCE OF SAFETY

At this point, I introduce the idea that it is my responsibility to be the primary keeper of safety, and I describe some of the ways we keep our work in the safe zone. The following sample script for presenting the first-session therapy map is a composite of several first-session conversations:

> *It is very important that we work in a way that feels safe to you. Though we will be working together to keep things safe, I will take more responsibility for that initially.*
>
> *One of the ways to promote safety is by how we will work. As I mentioned previously, rather than having you re-tell the experience, we will work on identifying its effects on your life, how to manage those effects, how to recover some commitments that may have been lost because of the experience, and then explore ways that you could live your life in a way that better matches your commitments and desires.*
>
> *Another way we do this work safely is using check-ins at the beginning and, more importantly, at the end of our session.*
>
> *A third way is by incorporating body-mind techniques. I include these because I have found that most people who are working*

to heal from trauma [The phrase "heal from trauma" should be replaced by whatever preferred description is a fit for the person (e.g., "reclaim one's life from abuse," "recover from the effects of hardship," etc.).] *have been impacted in a very physical way, not just mentally, emotionally, and spiritually.*

In a way, it is this intense physiological or body aspect that differentiates the less intrusive problems of life from traumatic ones. Is this the case for you? And does it make sense for your situation? [I have found that individuals working with the effects of trauma find this to be true for them, but I believe it is important to confirm with a check-in.]

[The individual verbally agrees.]

The way I include the body-mind piece is by offering you some tools or techniques for monitoring, managing, and integrating these physical aspects of the work. Learning these techniques and then integrating them into our conversation can be a useful way to keep the work in a place that is hopeful, productive, and safe. Perhaps more importantly, it is these techniques that help keep us away from falling into despair, hopelessness, and overwhelm—the all-too-common pitfalls of working with tremendous hardship.

Initially, as I am explaining these techniques to you, I will be doing much of the talking. However, once you get the gist of these ideas, it is important for you to edit, modify, change, delete, and basically customize these ideas to fit for you. That is, they work better when you can make them your own.

> *Once you are comfortable with doing that, my input tends to become quite minimal. As well, I am hoping that these strategies will be useful and doable in your day-to-day life. My hope is that they can become tools you have in your back pocket to use anytime and anyplace you might need them.*

To some, body-mind work is different, unconventional, and maybe even a bit odd. It is not just talking, which is the kind of therapy most people are familiar with; rather, it involves body pieces such as breath work, movement, or body scans. Because this kind of therapeutic conversation is not regular therapy fare, it is important during the first session to make sure the individual is aware of this piece and is comfortable with it.

Also, there is usually more of a question-and-answer format going on than what I have represented here. The individual's questions and comments guide the level of detail that I provide.

However, if any of the above points have not been addressed in a pre-therapy conversation, I will take extra time to do so in the first session. I have found that the more time I spend meticulously creating a safe working foundation in the early stages, the faster and easier the individual is able to move through the tough, complex work later on.

Introductory Therapy Maps:
Establishing the De-centred but Influential Relationship

PRE-THERAPY MAP	**FIRST-SESSION THERAPY MAP**
Purpose is to briefly outline the kind of service I can provide such that the individual can decide if it is a fit with what they are looking for.	Purpose is to briefly outline the service on offer and to create safety.
Does not require extra preparation. The conversation is intended to be short and informational in nature; it lends itself to being straightforward and matter of fact.	Create a sense of emotional safety by showing up to the session grounded and ready to hold a calm space. (See Chapter 3 for further discussion on therapist self-care ideas.)
Gain a rudimentary understanding of the individual's hopes and concerns for therapy.	Gain a rudimentary understanding of the individual's hopes and concerns for therapy.
Provide a description of my approach, touching on narrative practices, body-mind aspects, and a focus on safety. Keep this very brief. Include the idea that I do not see direct re-tellings of trauma as requisite for the work.	Provide a description of my approach, touching on narrative practices, body-mind aspects, and a focus on safety. Include the idea that I do not see direct re-tellings of trauma as requisite for the work.
Keep the conversation in the realm of information sharing only, making explicit that its purpose is to allow the individual to determine whether we are a good fit for therapy together.	Tie practices described above to the individual's reasons for coming to therapy (i.e., hopes and concerns). Invite questions and comments.

PRE-THERAPY MAP	FIRST-SESSION THERAPY MAP
Limit the conversation to 15–30 minutes. This keeps it in the information-sharing realm and out of the therapy realm.	Allow for extra time, especially if not preceded by a pre-therapy conversation or meet-and-greet session.
–	Introduce safety practices: breath work and therapy worries work (discussed in Chapter 2).
–	If time is on my side, begin mapping the effects of trauma. Chances are some of the effects have surfaced during the therapy worries work.

Introductory Therapy Maps in a Nutshell

To summarize, these maps serve to:

- Describe the collaborative (de-centred but influential) nature of the work in that the individual's ideas and knowledges are privileged and how that shifts with respect to safety aspects.
- Establish a check-in practice that sets the stage for future checking in.
- Introduce narrative methods of inquiry by using externalizing language.
- Introduce the idea of body-mind techniques.
- Outline the importance of safety and address the idea of direct re-tellings.

THE SOUND CHECK

Narrative ways of working have been my primary therapy lens for the past couple of decades, and I have had countless opportunities to practice holding a de-centred but influential stance. Despite this, I find creating and sustaining this stance requires considerable attention and energy. It can be a bit tricky at times, especially when working with trauma. Consequently, in order to resist the press to shift towards a more centred position, I have created a self-monitoring protocol that I have dubbed the Sound Check.

I was inspired to create this technique by observing the talented performing artists of the Calgary Folk Music Festival. As a folk-fest attendee, one of my favourite parts of the experience is watching the performing artists set up on stage. Because several artists often share one venue, sound checks tend to be interactive and elaborate affairs.

Typically, sound checks are conducted out of view of the audience prior to the performance; not so at the open outdoor stage of the folk festival. Anyone can wander up prior to a set and hang out while the musicians work through their sound check. Witnessing this process is pure magic to me. It feels like a sneak peek into the world of the performing artist.

There are the murmured evaluations and directives between performer and sound technician, followed by my favourite part: one of the vocalists says, "Check, che-e-eck, check, check, one, two, three, che-e-eck," repeatedly into the microphone. I love this bit. For me, it sums up all that preceded it and captures the ambiance of the sound check.

The performing artist is the main attraction, but the sound technician has a role to play as well. The quality of the performance hinges on ensuring the equipment is working properly and getting the mix just right. It is about collaboration. Or to quote singer-songwriter Stephen Fearing:

> The whole point of a sound check is to ensure and enhance clear, harmonious communication between the performer and audience as well as ensure that the performer can hear themselves clearly and accurately. Essentially, it is to make sure the PA [public address system] doesn't impede the performance and communication of musical ideas but [rather] enhances that transmission.[16]

I have been fascinated by the back-and-forth of these precise adjustments—the attuning to vocals, the calibration of equipment, the intense focus and care. And all of this effort and attention are for the express purpose of ensuring that the audience receives the highest quality experience possible.

At some point, it struck me: there is a parallel to the therapy context. The performing artist brings the lyrics and the melody to the stage much like the individual brings their life stories and their lived experiences to the session. The sound technician works behind the scenes, striving to perfect the integrity of the performance just as I strive to sustain the therapeutic conversation. And so inspired, I now strive to emulate in my work the care taken by those consummate performers and technicians.

I imagine the person I am working with as the performing artist, and I am the sound technician. Together we share the role of audience, and between the two of us, we figure out a "mix" that

16 Stephen Fearing in an email communication, October 12, 2022.

works. "Check, che-e-eck, check" becomes my internalized therapist mantra.

And the analogy does not stop there. The musicianspeak[17] during the sound check aptly parallels the therapeutic process:

- "The vocals sound woofy [too many low–mid frequencies]."
  THERAPY PARALLEL: Therapist comments are off track.

- "Could I get some more volume? How about more reverb [creates space around the sound]?"
  THERAPY PARALLEL: Therapist gives the person the time and space to respond to questions.

- "Am I in the house [checking if the artist's voice is coming through on the main PA system]?"
  THERAPY PARALLEL: Is the individual's voice being privileged rather than the therapist's?

- "I think these monitors are out of phase [two speakers hooked up incorrectly such that the sound they are creating is confusing and misrepresenting what you are putting into them]."
  THERAPY PARALLEL: Therapist's editorializing is off track.

The Sound Check is a self-monitoring exercise that helps me to self-correct when I am becoming too centred (Part 1) and to enhance or amplify when I am in a more de-centred position (Part 2).

---

17 Credit goes to Stephen Fearing for explaining to me this process and its related terminology.

Sound Check Part 1

Check. Check. Check. Finding the right mix. This is the corrective part of my check-in. I look for warning signals that indicate I have strayed from the de-centred but influential balance that I want. Then, I endeavour to adjust by turning up certain aspects of my practice and muting others. I tweak whichever parts of my conversation and presentation seem off or a bit wonky.

Some common warning signals include:

- I am talking too much.
- I am sharing my own personal experiences in a way that is privileging my experience rather than the individual's.
- I am using directive language rather than questioning, open-ended language.
- I am making assumptions about what the individual means rather than asking about the meaning and allowing the individual to elaborate.
- I notice that my inner Columbo[18] has wandered off. That is, I feel myself moving away from a place of playful curiosity to a place where I am making assumptions.

Sound Check Part 2

Check. Check. Check. Finding the groove. Hopefully, I only have to do minor adjustments after Part 1. Then, I can shift my focus to what is working and amplify those aspects.

---

18 Columbo is a quirky, fictional TV detective played by Peter Falk. He is famous for his disarming style of questioning characterized by a stance of open curiosity. His use of questioning to expose the modus operandi of the culprits parallels the type of questioning used in Narrative Practice to expose the modus operandi of problems. Calling on my "inner Columbo" helps me to bolster this type of curiosity.

Some signals that I am in a de-centred position include:

- I am inquiring about the person's impressions, feelings, commitments, and values rather than making observations, judgments, or pronouncements about what I think they are.
- Instead of offering my own impressions, I am asking questions and reflecting (or editorializing) on the individual's answers.
- I am feeling genuinely curious about the individual's answers to my questions; I have an expectation that the individual will uncover something new and particular.
- I am quelling and suppressing any assumptions I have about what the individual is feeling, thinking, or experiencing.
- I find myself being surprised by some of the individual's comments; my curiosity is piqued.
- When I do ask a question, make an editorializing statement, or provide any kind of input, I check in with the individual regarding its helpfulness or relevance. Following is a list of some possible check-in questions:

    - "Is this question helpful?"
    - "Does this comment make sense to you?"
    - "Am I understanding what you are trying to tell me?" (Or as one charming adolescent once teasingly said to me, "You mean, are you picking up what I'm laying down?")

- I am doing overall check-ins to ensure that we are on track by asking things like "Is this the kind of thing you were hoping for from our work today?"

    - If the individual's answers to any of my check-in queries show that I have wandered off track, then I make the necessary adjustments. It's not enough to just check in. I need to follow through and make the adjustments. And then check again.

- I am connecting our current work back to the initial conversation where the individual identified what they wanted to gain from our work together.

For the purpose of explanation, I have written the Sound Check piece as quite linear: Part 1 and Part 2. In reality, just as is the case for an artist during a live performance, the therapist is moving between both self-monitoring and adjustments throughout the course of a session. Regardless, the Sound Check metaphor serves as a useful tool for me in supporting the expression of a de-centred but influential position.

Concluding Thoughts

I see the de-centred but influential relationship as being the bedrock of effective trauma therapy. It provides the solid and safe foundation for the work. I have described how I endeavour to lay the foundation for this type of connection with the individual. And though the focus on safety adds complexity to the development of the de-centred but influential position, I believe it is vital for creating and sustaining a strong enough foundation for this type of work.

At the onset, I see the relationship as an aggregate of both de-centred pieces and centred pieces. The de-centred bits are that, first, the individuals' experiences and knowledges are privileged and form the centrepiece of the therapeutic conversation. Second, what individuals say trumps what I, the practitioner, say at any given moment in the conversation. They get to say no to the direction, content, or pace of our conversation, and I will follow their lead (in-the-moment power and control). Third, the individuals get to know what I plan to offer them, which gives them the opportunity to evaluate and make decisions in advance regarding their participation in the plan (power and control over the bigger, long-term picture).

The more centred bits are that I have something of value to offer the individuals on their change journey, namely expertise and special knowledges about safe ways of working with trauma through certain narrative practices and body-mind techniques. The mindful integration of these sometimes-disparate aspects allows me to create a foundation both flexible and strong enough to support individuals as they embark on the profoundly challenging work of healing from trauma.

CHAPTER 2

Safety Tools for the Individual

I CLEARLY REMEMBER THE DAY when I stumbled briefly into enlightenment and found the missing safety piece of the how-*do*-I-do-this puzzle. It was the day that my sister-in-law Janet asked me to be her practice subject for a new coaching technique that she was learning called Belief Re-patterning.[19]

Janet is a coach and facilitator with a master's degree in adult education and counselling; she uses her expertise to support businesses with their management practices. For one of her training courses, she was required to accumulate a certain number of practice hours. In me, she had found an eager participant.

She explained the coaching technique and showed me a card with the steps of what we were about to do. My brain clicked in, immediately slotting my narrative practice template over it. "So far, so good," I thought. "I can relate to this."

Janet walked me through the problem-solving technique, which involved helping the individual create supportive statements (my narrative practice equivalent: helping the individual uncover preferred understandings) and pairing these with breath work.

19 Casey, S. (2012). *Belief re-patterning: The amazing technique for "flipping the switch" to positive thoughts*. Hay House Insights.

As we started to work through the problem-solving steps, I realized that the type of wording and turn of phrase used to create the supportive statements was, narratively speaking, mostly externalizing language. In this method, like in Narrative Practice, the problem was viewed as the problem; the person was not the problem. Again, I thought, "I get this. I like this. This is my kind of thing."

Janet then introduced the idea of adding breath work to accompany the newly constructed statements. This addition of taking a breath after stating one of the supportive statements seemed to help me solidify the learning/problem-solving process. It made the idea feel more settled somehow.

It was this idea of using breath work embedded in the problem-solving conversation that was the practice piece I was looking for. I was able to conceptualize how I could incorporate breath work into the narrative therapy conversation.

Up to this point, I had been seeking a therapeutic method that would address the physiological activation that is often such a powerful and distressing accompaniment to the trauma experience. In my search for this, I had explored and received training in several areas such as hypnosis, relaxation techniques, mindfulness meditation, cranial sacral therapy, neuropsychology, and yoga. All of these disciplines speak to the role of the breath in understanding the body-mind connection.

It was the work of mindfulness proponents like Jon Kabat-Zinn,[20] Daniel Siegel,[21,22] and others that led me further along the path of incorporating breath work practices to create safety. By tying the recent findings of neuroscience and interpersonal biology to the ancient wisdom of meditation practices, these proponents of mindfulness have enriched the understanding of the mechanisms of self-regulation.

That is, in applying a scientific lens to a person's state of being, they described how the person's central nervous system manages self-regulation. (For an in-depth discussion, see Stephen W. Porges's work.[23])

The ideas that resonated for my work were those that explained the workings of the autonomic nervous system—in particular, the parasympathetic and sympathetic branches—and how it responds to stress or danger.

Simply put, the autonomic nervous system is responsible for regulating a range of involuntary bodily functions such as heart rate and respiration. The sympathetic branch of this system (SNS) is responsible for activating certain bodily functions in the face of a perceived threat or danger. This is referred to as the fight-or-flight response.

When activated, the SNS sets off a myriad of bodily reactions—such as increased heart rate and respiration, for example—all of which are designed to prepare the individual to take action

20 Kabat-Zinn, J. (2009). *Full catastrophe living: Using the wisdom of your body and mind to face stress, pain and illness*. Bantam Dell.

21 Siegel, D. (2010). *The mindful therapist: A clinician's guide to mindsight and neural integration*. W.W. Norton.

22 Siegel. D. (2012). *Pocket guide to interpersonal neurobiology: An integrative handbook of the mind*. W.W. Norton.

23 Porges, S. (2011). *The polyvagal theory: Neurophysiological foundations of emotions, attachment, communication and regulation*. W.W. Norton.

against the perceived threat. Feelings of tension, anxiety, and panic are associated with this type of activation.

Conversely, the parasympathetic branch of the nervous system (PNS) serves an inhibitory function. When activated, this system sets off bodily reactions such as decreased heart rate, vigilance, and respiration. This is known as the rest-and-digest state. Feelings of calm and relaxation are associated with this type of activation.

Of particular interest to me was the idea that faster, shallower patterns of breathing are associated with agitation and/or excitation (SNS fight-or-flight states of being) and that slower, deeper patterns of breathing are associated with rest and/or relaxation (certain PNS states of being). I saw breathing as a key that could potentially unlock the ability to manage the agitation that can occur during therapy.

In other words, what I learned about breath work from my experiences with yoga and meditation had been consolidated and further elaborated upon by modern science. The upshot of this was my determination to develop a breath-work method whereby individuals would be able to regulate their own physiological response as we worked, which would in turn allow them to be more in charge of their own safety.

That day with Janet was the culmination of my quest to find a way to do talking therapy that would help individuals keep themselves feeling safe and, in particular, reduce (and ideally avoid) re-traumatization.

Body-Mind Safety: Breath Work and Check-Ins

Initially, I struggled to integrate some of these ideas directly into my therapy practice. When I attempted to do so, the session often had a stop-and-start feel to it. We would start the therapeutic conversation, the person would experience anxiety or agitation, we would stop and do one of the techniques to address this, and then we would restart the therapeutic conversation. For example, we might start with a conversation about mapping the effects of trauma, then we might move into doing a mindfulness meditation (or some form of breath work practice), and then we would return to mapping the effects.

I believe these types of sessions were useful, but they were missing the kind of flow and integrated quality for which I was searching. I wanted to be able to incorporate the body piece *within* the therapeutic conversation rather than just bookending it on either side.

As the upsetting (or "triggering") ideas arose in the therapeutic conversation along with the accompanying disruptive physiological response, I wanted to have the body-mind tools at hand for the individual to address these aspects in the moment. I wanted a method that would work with the body sensations (physiological) in synchrony with those understandings of the mind (cognitive) to which they were linked.

To this end, the method needed to do more than soothe the body's agitation. I also needed it to help individuals transform their body agitation into a different and *preferred bodily response* while simultaneously helping them to create a different and *preferred cognitive reconstruction* of the upsetting ideas. The meaning-making had to include making sense of the body piece in conjunction with the associated mind pieces. The method had to incorporate a whole lot of different pieces all at once.

The body-inclusion method I was seeking also had to fit with my narrative approach. I needed to incorporate it within the narrative practices (e.g., externalizing and re-authoring conversations) that, for me, are so key to this kind of work.

I found that many of the body-mind techniques I checked out tended to be quite top-down. That is, they required specialized expertise and knowledge that the therapist would use to deliver the technique to the individual in a directive manner. They tended to be more therapist centred than what I wanted. Because of this, the individual could not really expect to do this kind of work independently—at least, not without a fair bit of training first.

For example, hypnosis and traditional de-sensitization training can be useful tools for working with trauma, but their efficacy derives from a more expert-driven place than what I was seeking. I wanted to bring to the therapeutic experience a way of teaching safety techniques that would be more compatible with the de-centred but influential therapist position.

As well, I wanted to provide safety tools that individuals could master fairly quickly and with relative ease such that they could independently access them both inside and outside the therapy session. In other words, I was looking to integrate safety practices into methods of narrative inquiry in ways that optimize the individual's personal agency. I was striving to create user-friendly body-mind techniques that would be respectful of narrative practices, and that the individual could learn and use in our work together and eventually in the challenges of daily life.

What I ended up doing was systematically incorporating breath work techniques and specific safety-oriented therapy practices into and around externalizing and re-authoring conversations. It is a combination that I have found to be potent in supporting individuals to heal from traumatic experiences in a safe and often releasing—sometimes even joyous—manner.

The main safety pieces that I integrate with the narrative practices are:

- **THE BREATH WORK**—two types that I call restorative and constructive
- **THE 5-MINUTE BREATHING TASK**—an application of restorative breath work
- **THERAPY WORRIES WORK**—an application of constructive breath work
- **SAFETY CHECK-INS**—a kind of brief, informal safety screening

All of these practices are introduced in the early stages of therapy (i.e., during the first couple of meetings) with the idea of building a solid, strong, and safe therapeutic structure—a structure that rests upon the foundation of the de-centred but influential relationship.

Practices for Developing the Individual's Safety Tools

THE BREATH WORK

As mentioned above, my work with individuals who are dealing with the effects of trauma led me to the conclusion that safety during the therapeutic process required breath work that would not only calm bodily agitation but also assist individuals in transforming their distressing physiological and cognitive responses into preferred intentional understandings. To achieve this, I have found that more than one type of breath work is needed—a basic practice that soothes the body and a more complex practice that helps to integrate meaning. To that end, I have incorporated two main types of breath work practice: restorative and constructive.

Restorative Breath Work

I see this type of breath work as a basic self-management tool. There are many examples of this kind of breath work found in the mindfulness and yogic traditions. (See Resources for a list of books on yoga-related breath work.) I call this breath work restorative because its main purpose is to restore a sense of calm and, more importantly, safety to the body.

I have found it to be helpful to the individual for managing the internal physiological alarm system that is so readily triggered when working with the effects of trauma. That is, it allows individuals to soothe their physical self, which in turn enables them to maintain their composure so they can proceed more effectively with the hard work of therapy.

The management of upsetting physical sensations as they arise—not so much the upsetting thoughts and their content—is the primary focus here. In other words, this breath work directly addresses problems with dysregulation; or conversely, it works to help restore regulation. Distressing thoughts may be observed and acknowledged but not *reconstructed* in this type of breath work. Rather, the physiological sensations that accompany the emotion are the focus of attention.

I introduce the restorative breath work in the early stages of therapy. I tend to use it in a kind of stop-and-start fashion. That is, the individual puts the therapeutic conversation on hold while they are doing this kind of breath work and then resumes the therapeutic conversation once they have achieved a degree of physical equilibrium.

Restorative breath work is helpful in that once one has learned the basics of how to do it, it naturally evolves into a self-monitoring system. In other words, it teaches individuals to be aware of their pattern of breathing and to notice any changes in that breathing pattern, a change that could signal the beginning of upset or agitation. Moving forwards, the individual can use restorative breath work as needed. In short, it is a handy tool to help keep oneself feeling safe throughout the therapeutic process and beyond.

Safety benefits of this type of breath work are:

- Settling the body
- Calming the mind
- Providing clarity for the mind
- Helping to create a solid physical foundation, a feeling of groundedness from which to approach tough work

- Enhancing the ability to recover a sense of safety (or composure) as needed
- Allowing one to monitor one's level of comfort and safety
- Contributing to a greater sense of personal power over the effects of trauma

AN APPLICATION OF RESTORATIVE BREATH WORK: THE 5-MINUTE BREATHING TASK

As mentioned, restorative breath work falls under the umbrella of mindfulness: the individual takes an observational stance on what is going on in the mind and body and, from a nonjudgmental place, invokes breathing techniques for the purpose of inviting calm. It is a safety measure that lends itself well to being cultivated both inside and outside the therapy session. As such, it can be very helpful in supporting the individual to persevere with the sometimes-daunting process of trauma therapy, especially in the early stages of this work.

I often briefly introduce breath work during the first meeting with individuals. I have found that those individuals who are unfamiliar with breath work concepts appreciate a more detailed explanation of how to do restorative breath work.

To address this, I developed a restorative tool called the 5-Minute Breathing Task. In developing this task, I have drawn primarily from the work of integrated medicine expert Andrew Weil[24] and mindfulness expert Jon Kabat-Zinn,[25] as well as from the yogic traditions.

24 Weil, A. (1999). *Breathing: The master key to self healing*. [Audio CDs]. Sounds True.

25 Greater Good Science Center. (2010, April 14). *Jon Kabat-Zinn: What is mindfulness?* [Video]. You Tube. https://www.youtube.com/watch?v=xoLQ3qkhOwO.

The 5-Minute Breathing Task involves measuring and monitoring one's breathing rate. It is a simple but useful exercise that involves counting one's breaths before and after the completion of a three-minute period of "calm" breathing. It provides an opportunity to develop body and breath awareness, and it also teaches people the kind of breathing patterns that are conducive to a more relaxed or calmer state of being. (See Appendix A for a detailed description of the 5-Minute Breathing Task.)

It is my experience that many people who have been struggling with high levels of anxiety or distress for long periods of time tend to have a base breathing rate that is excessively elevated and to breathe in a manner that is shallow and rapid. That is, individuals report that anxiety as expressed by an elevated breathing rate is showing up in their everyday life. This "keyed up" kind of breathing often becomes, in a sense, their normal. Consequently, for those individuals wishing to reduce the influence of anxiety, the 5-Minute Breathing Task is often a useful tool for them.

Also, it is this steady, slower, belly breathing that is effective for use with the breath work component during the later therapy sessions. In other words, this breathing task also provides a scaffold that facilitates the learning of more complex breath work practices (i.e., constructive breath work) when the therapeutic conversation is added into the mix.

Before explaining the 5-Minute Breathing Task, I often provide some background about how it works. This introduction is dependent on the knowledge, skills, and expertise that the person brings to the session. Some individuals have quite an expansive knowledge about body and breath work; others have little to none. I endeavour to customize the information for the particular individual.

For example, 17-year-old Cory, who had taken extensive yoga teacher training, required about 30 seconds of explanation before he fully embraced this technique. He was familiar with different kinds of breath work and how they could be used as a tool for body awareness and for directing his intentions. In fact, he already had established a daily practice of doing this on his own. Little-to-no explanation was required here.

However, 48-year-old businessman Tom, who admitted that he found his wife's new age interests (a category in which he included yoga and meditation) off-putting, required a more science-based explanation. A brief explanation of the parasympathetic and sympathetic responses of the central nervous system and how breath work can play a role in learning to better balance oneself between these two types of responses was a helpful framework for him.

Many of the children and adolescents with whom I have worked have some knowledge of these concepts. However, many people, even if they have an understanding of the body science of breathing, do not have much experience with actually using their breath to make themselves feel better. Furthermore, I have found that many people who have tried out breath techniques (e.g., mindfulness meditation) understand that these practices can be effective but have difficulty integrating them into their everyday lives in a consistent manner.

I find this difficulty understandable because developing a mindfulness practice requires energy, time, focus, and discipline. People who are coming to therapy for trauma work are usually emotionally exhausted and stressed, the casualties of which are often those very things: energy, time, focus, and discipline.

Consequently, my hope in developing a mindful breathing task was to make it as simple and quick as possible while still being effective. The 5-Minute Breathing Task meets these criteria. It breaks down the skill of doing mindfulness meditation into smaller, more manageable chunks.

Gaining some mastery with this task also acts as a bridge for individuals to then try other more involved mindfulness techniques. More importantly to the therapeutic context, it allows the individual to gain a skill that will help them navigate the trauma work in a safer manner.

I have included in Appendix A a copy of the 5-Minute Breathing Task handout that I created for individuals to take home with them. It includes much of what I might say to someone in a session when introducing this practice.

It is important to note that I only provide the handout once I have ascertained that the individual understands and has gained a measure of comfort with the task. This is to ensure that the individual experiences some success with it when they attempt it on their own. Otherwise, failure with the task can lead to frustration and anxiety around breath work that could be detrimental to the therapeutic process.

Generally, I introduce the 5-Minute Breathing Task whenever an individual has expressed a desire to create more calm. However, with trauma therapy, I am moving towards offering this task during earlier sessions as it aids in evaluating and then addressing the level of comfort or distress. Also, those individuals who have identified high anxiety as one of the effects of the trauma experience often really appreciate this exercise.

Ultimately, the 5-Minute Breathing Task is a stand-alone tool for the individual to learn and use outside of the therapy sessions.

It is the kind of technique that is easy to learn and then assimilate into day-to-day life.

Constructive Breath Work

I see this type of breath work as primarily a meaning-making and meaning-integration tool. It is the technique that I have developed specifically to address the safety issues particular to highly charged traumatic material. Constructive breath work, in combination with narrative therapy practices, is a large part of the answer to my original question of "How do I help an individual heal from the effects of trauma without re-traumatization?"

From a narrative therapy standpoint, constructive breath work facilitates the safe integration and transformation of the old problem story to the new preferred story and does so both cognitively and physiologically. The primary focus of *restorative* breath work is working with the physical (bodily sensations); its main purpose is to calm or soothe the body. In contrast, the primary focus of *constructive* breath work is working with the cognitions of the mind; its main purpose is the integration of preferred meanings and understandings with the body.

Constructive breath work is more complex than restorative breath work. This is primarily because its focus is meaning-making, which is a multi-layered and complex process in and of itself. Secondly, constructive breath work is more complex because it is focusing on the integration of information on two fronts simultaneously: body and mind.

To reiterate, with this technique, individuals use the breath work to craft, punctuate, and solidify the new preferred understanding that they have constructed, *and* they use it to construct a new, preferred physiological response to accompany this new understanding. That is, a new connection between a preferred meaning of trauma (in the mind) and a preferred physiological response to trauma (in the body) is forged.

While restorative breath takes a break from the main therapeutic conversation, constructive breath work is embedded within the therapeutic conversation. However, constructive breath work serves a similar function as restorative breath work in that it also offers a way to monitor the body's status. It is yet another way for the individual to tune into the body's early warning signs of danger. This, in turn, allows the individual to make adjustments in the moment, thereby preserving the safety of the work.

Though I originally developed constructive breath work specifically to accompany the core trauma work (illustrated in Chapter 6), I have found it to be effective for other types of therapeutic conversations. It is useful for any therapeutic work where the individual is creating new, preferred understandings, especially when there is an accompanying emotional charge. I present examples of these types of therapeutic conversations in Chapter 4.

Constructive breath work enhances therapeutic safety in ways that parallel restorative breath work. Like restorative breath work, constructive breath work settles the body, calms the mind, and so on. However, constructive breath work adds an additional and vital safety piece that is beyond the scope of restorative breath work. It assists the individual in reworking highly charged material without becoming overwhelmed or re-traumatized by the process.

AN APPLICATION OF CONSTRUCTIVE BREATH WORK: ADDRESSING THERAPY WORRIES

Over time, I learned that individuals brought several worries to their first session that were indirectly related to the presenting concern. These worries sprang from a range of sources: a Sense of Immediacy, All-or-Nothing Thinking, and a Fear of Failure and Setbacks being the most common.

It is these change-process worries that I use as a vehicle for introducing the constructive breath work technique. This application of constructive breath work occurs in a therapeutic conversation that externalizes these worries and uses the breath work to systematically identify and transform any undesirable beliefs that get in the way of the intended work. In this context, individuals learn and practice the breath work technique on relatively safe yet relevant material.

First, therapy worries are relatively safe material because they are not directly associated with the trauma or abuse for which the individuals are seeking help. As such, this material usually does not come with as high an emotional charge, and thus, it is easier to manage. Secondly, therapy worries are relevant in that they pertain to what gets in the way of working on the problem of interest.

For me, taking the time to address therapy worries has become an integral part of doing trauma therapy. This kind of therapeutic conversation is a useful safety practice on its own. It also acts as a scaffold for learning the constructive breath work technique, a safety practice that is key to the successful navigation of the later more challenging core trauma work.

Though therapy worries can be viewed as an effect of the trauma experience, the individual has not, at this point, explicitly identified them as such because we have not yet begun the work of mapping the effects. Nonetheless, I can refer back to the ideas explored during this conversation as starting points for exploring the effects of abuse/hardship later. Thus, this therapy worries conversation can also provide a scaffold for later externalizing conversations.

Following is an example of how I might introduce a therapy worries conversation:

> *Almost always, I have found that people bring some worries and fears to the first session that feed into feelings of discomfort or unease. That is, often there are thoughts or ideas about even starting therapy or doing the therapy that can get in the way. Is this the case for you?*
>
> [The individual verbally agrees.]
>
> *I would like to introduce the breath work techniques to you by working with these worries and fears first. Does that make sense to you?*
>
> [The individual verbally agrees.]

I acknowledge that one of the primary tenets of Narrative Therapy is to avoid making assumptions about the individual's experience. Genuine curiosity is the rule. However, in the name of safety, I am assuming that addressing these kinds of worries is relevant to the individual. Nonetheless, I endeavour to check-in with individuals about their position on this idea by asking if it makes sense and if it is okay to proceed with this kind of work.

Even if I am quite sure that this must be true for the individual, I believe it is still important to ask. It allows the person a chance to pause and take a position on the work that is about to unfold, even if it is a position of agreement. Also, it is the taking of that position, the acknowledgement and understanding that there is choice in this work, that provides the template for future check-ins.

Next, I introduce some common issues that others in the past have brought to work on with me (also known as insider knowledge) by saying something like the following:

> *Some common worries, doubts, fears, and concerns that others have encountered in this work, which can get in the way of moving forwards with the work, are:*
>
> - *"I have to fix everything right away today or soon after today."* [An example of a tremendous Sense of Immediacy]
> - *"If I don't fix all the concerns associated with this issue, then I am a failure."* [An example of All-or-Nothing Thinking]
> - *"I will fail in my attempts to resolve my problem. I will remain stuck in the same place. Things may even get worse."* [An example of Fear of Failure and Setbacks]
> - *"This problem has been around a long time and has been a huge problem for me. Therefore it must inevitably take a long time to shift it or feel some relief from it."* [An example of Problem History Logic]
> - *"Working with trauma and hardship means I have to go into the dark place, the 'pit of despair,' in order to heal*

> *from that despair. This kind of work has to be long, relentless, arduous, and despairing work."* [An example of Problem Intensity Logic]

Then, I ask one or more of the following questions:

> *Do any of these ideas/worries resonate for you?*
>
> *Do you find that these thoughts are the kind of thoughts that can stop you in your tracks and might be preventing you from moving forwards with respect to healing from trauma and hardship? Or might they be getting in the way of you heading in the right direction?*
>
> *Do you find that though these ideas/worries may have originated from a place of protecting you, they may have outlived their usefulness and are now exerting too much unwanted influence on your ability to heal, change, and move on from the effects of trauma and hardship?*

Finally, I ask the individual if they would like to learn the breath work technique using the worries that they identified:

> *Are you okay with doing some breath work around them to help reduce their influence on you?*

When individuals answer in the affirmative, they will then tell me which ones are relevant. Then, I introduce the breath work in more detail:

Okay, so now I would like to show you the body-mind breath technique that will support our work together. [I prefer to use the term body-mind rather than mind-body in order to draw attention to the greater emphasis of the body piece in this kind of work.] *Initially, I will do a lot of the talking to explain how this works, but it works best when you customize it and change it up for your own uses.*

In a nutshell, it involves saying statements aloud in combination with slow, long, full breaths. The intention is to both calm the body and clear the mind, which then helps you to put to rest certain worries you might be holding about this work. That is, the breath work helps to calm the mind, which in turn allows you to focus on problem-solving and creating preferred counterstatements.

We will first identify a worry, an idea, or even an image that you suspect is getting in the way for you. Then we will create a preferred response aimed at reducing or changing its hindering impact. In other words, you are identifying the ideas you don't want and reducing their influence. Then, you are creating the ideas you want to privilege instead.

Most people, when they are first learning how to use the breath work, find it hard to come up with their own preferred statements. I have collected some of these kinds of statements from others that we can use as a starting point. However, if you do already have some statements in mind, that's super. What is important for you to know is that you hold the veto card here. My job is to come up with some good guesses about types of statements. Your job is to change them or decline them as you see fit.

We will start by looking at the list of unhelpful worries that other people doing this kind of work have brought to their first session. If the worry resonates with you, let me know, and then together, we will come up with a preferred counterstatement to that worry.

Once we have crafted a statement to your satisfaction, you will say it aloud and take a deep belly or "Buddha" breath. I will do the breathing part along with you. You then sit for a few seconds and just notice what—if any—thoughts or images come to your mind and what—if any—sensations show up in your body.

If some bodily tension or doubts or inner protests have arisen following your counterstatement, then we address those in a similar fashion. If you feel a sense of calmness and rightness or ease with no doubts arising, then we move on to the next concern. Make sense?

[The individual verbally agrees.]

Also, it's okay to forget the statement that we have just created. It is my job to do the remembering of the words. So, if you forget, I will tell you. I have found that whenever people are working on emotional or stressful issues, it is common for them to get foggy in the middle of it, and that fogginess makes them forget the particular words. That is why I will be responsible for remembering the statements. It's as if I am the understudy for your character in a play. I feed you the lines you want to say if you have drawn a blank, but they are your lines.

These worry thoughts can create a kind of static or block that gets in the way of our work. Using the breath work when addressing these thoughts helps to settle or disperse this interference, creating more clarity and ease in the mind so we can focus on the rest of our work. It is a kind of mindfulness housecleaning that removes the clutter left by these kinds of worries. It may seem a bit awkward or odd at first. Eventually, it becomes easy to move in and out of this practice depending on what comes up in our conversation. You ready to try it out?

[The individual verbally agrees.]

Once the individual has decided which ideas are problematic for them, we begin the work of crafting a counterstatement that they feel is supportive and want to embrace instead of the worry idea.

Again, as this is still a learning process for the individual, I scaffold that learning by providing some statements to choose from that I have gathered from previous individuals' work. The idea is that we work together with the preferred counterstatement to make it fit for the individual, and once they are comfortable with it, they say it aloud and take a breath in.

Preferred Counterstatement Examples

The following are some examples of preferred ideas from conversations with individuals who externalized a range of fears and worries. In a session, I would not present all of these to the individual. However, I try to present at least one idea from each of the categories, and I always include one example from the category of Problem Intensity Logic.

To address a Sense of Immediacy and All-or-Nothing Thinking:

1. I understand and I am okay with the fact that I don't have to fix everything right away. <breath>
2. I can honour my own pace of change. <breath>
3. I am okay with taking small steps, knowing that small steps can lead to big changes. <breath>

To address the Fear of Failure and Setbacks:

1. I recognize that fears and anxiety about not moving forwards are all part of the learning, and I am up for this learning. <breath>
2. I know that this learning might not be steady and that I may encounter setbacks. However, I am ready to find ways to get back on track more quickly after a setback. <breath>
3. I have experienced setbacks with regard to Problem X or Concern Y before, and I have been able to come back from some of those setbacks. I did it when A, B, C happened. And I know that I can use that knowledge and experience to help me right now in moving forwards. <breath>

To address the Problem History Logic:

1. I can be open to the idea that just because a problem has been around for a long time does not mean it has to take a long time before I can make some significant change with regard to the problem. <breath>
2. I can consider the idea that even if the problem has been around a long time, I can find some relief from it in a relatively short time. <breath>
3. Even though this problem and its effects have been around a really long time, I am open to the idea that I can take some important steps in reducing the impact of this problem in a relatively short time. <breath>

To address the Problem Intensity Logic (Trauma or Tremendous Hardship Logic):

1. I can be open to learning ways to keep this work on the side of hopeful work and away from the despairing, the overwhelming, or the hopeless side of work. <breath>
2. I am not afraid of hard work. I can do hard work. It is hopeless, despairing, and overwhelming work that I do not want to do. I can be open to doing hard work that is on the hopeful, gratifying side of things. <breath>
3. I have fallen into the despairing, overwhelming, and hopeless place with regard to this issue (e.g., trauma/abuse/hardship) in the past, and I have been able to get out of that place. I acknowledge that I am ready to learn more and/or better ways to take myself out of that disturbing place should I find myself back there again. <breath>

I have found that individuals quickly respond to certain themes and statements and readily jump into the work of creating their own statements. The order of which worries to address first is determined by the individual. Some of the worries or fears are easily diffused, and others require the development of several preferred statements. It is different for each person. (See Appendix B for more examples of these types of statements.)

What has been a common theme is the value that individuals have placed on addressing these fears and worries associated with doing the work of healing from trauma. In my recollection, all individuals to whom I have presented these ideas have found that one or more resonated for them. That is, there seems to be some consensus that these therapy worries are around, that they do get in the way of the intended work, and that it is useful to address them.

I have found that the more time and attention I place on addressing this therapy anxiety, the more quickly and smoothly the rest of the therapeutic process unfolds. This is important safety work, and the safer the individual feels prior to embarking on intense trauma therapy, the more effective and positive that work will be.

As well, though it is important to address therapy worries before jumping into trauma work, these kinds of worries can make an appearance at any time during the healing journey. Accordingly, some individuals choose to revisit this kind of work periodically throughout their sessions. (See Chapter 4 for an illustration of this.)

Once the individual and I have concluded the therapy worries work, I check in again and ask which counterstatements resonated the most for them. Then, I ask the individual to write them down or at least identify them as I write them down. I make sure the individual has a copy of these key breath work statements so they can use them at home. In this way, the individual creates a bank of grounding, self-soothing breath work statements that they can access at any time. I see this as a helpful way for individuals to support the continuing development of their preferred story.

AN EXAMPLE OF CONSTRUCTIVE BREATH WORK: ADDRESSING JULIA'S THERAPY WORRIES

Following is an example of the breath work taken from a session with Julia, a woman who initiated therapy with me in order to address the mental health concerns that she associated with the sexual abuse she had experienced as a child. Julia chose to address three different therapy worries:

1. **SENSE OF IMMEDIACY** says that she has to figure everything out right away. Julia's counterstatements to this worry were as follows:

    a. "I can honour my own pace of healing." <breath>
    b. "I don't have to sort everything today, right now." <breath>
    c. "I grant myself patience and kindness in the healing process." <breath>

2. **PROBLEM INTENSITY LOGIC** says that healing from the effects of sexual abuse requires her to go back into the "pit of despair." Julia's counterstatements to this worry were as follows:

a "I can be open to the idea that it is possible for me to do hard work to heal from abuse that is hopeful work." <breath>

b "I can be open to the idea that doing despairing kinds of work can be avoided." <breath>

3 **PROBLEM HISTORY LOGIC** says that because a difficult problem has been around a long time, it inevitably takes an equally long time before she can find any significant resolution or gain some measure of relief from it. Julia's counterstatement to this worry was as follows:

a "I can be open to the idea that I can acquire some degree of relief or resolution about my issues in a relatively short time." <breath>

The idea that effective change regarding a presenting problem is possible in only a few sessions is a possibility I often share with individuals when tackling worries about pace of change. I recognize that in sharing this idea, I am doing so from a more centred position. However, in the early stages of the therapy process, I believe this is warranted as I see this idea as useful in bolstering safety, which is primarily my responsibility at this juncture.

Julia chose not to work with the Fear of Failure and Setbacks. However, work with individuals facing similar kinds of hardship has led me to the belief that addressing this worry early on is a very useful safety measure.

If I could rewind time, I would have asked Julia if this was a concern for her. A preferred counterstatement to this worry could be:

> I know I can come back from setbacks. I've done it before, and I can do it again should I encounter a setback during this particular time of healing. <breath>

In suggesting this, I would have been stepping more towards the centred end of the de-centred but influential continuum. But again, at this stage, I believe this shift is warranted for the purposes of establishing safety.

After working through these worrisome beliefs with the accompanying breath work, Julia remarked that she felt a great sense of relief and calm with regard to proceeding with therapy. She marvelled at how powerful this initial work was for her. By addressing these therapy worries in this manner, Julia was already experiencing more hope and relief in connection to the abuse than she could remember feeling in a very long time.

Essentially, during this brief focus on therapy worry thoughts, she had been able to create some results for herself right away. It was immediate, positive evidence that she was capable of achieving some measure of relief despite the long history associated with her presenting concern.

This experience infused her with a sense of hope and possibility and energized her subsequent work. It provided a solid platform from which we were then able to safely move into externalizing and re-authoring conversations (described in Chapter 4) about the effects of childhood sexual abuse.

When and How to Use the Breath Work

As my work has evolved, I have found the use of breath work to be particularly useful in the following therapeutic contexts:

- Aiding the individual to keep their body feeling safe and calm by identifying and addressing distress that starts to surface throughout counselling. That is, using restorative breath work techniques is a way to preempt and manage triggers.
- Addressing the individual's fears, worries, and discomfort related to doing the work by using constructive breath work in therapy worries conversations at the outset of counselling.
- Consolidating the individual's profound insights or new learnings. When the person has had an epiphany or breakthrough understanding, constructive breath work can help to capture this and punctuate it.
- Reworking the individual's emotionally laden and physiologically charged thoughts and ideas about the trauma experience—that is, using constructive breath work with the absent but implicit inquiry of the core trauma work.
- Providing the individual with a set of self-management tools—both restorative and constructive breath work techniques—that they can take and use in day-to-day life outside of the counselling session.
- Incorporating it anytime the individual thinks it would be a good idea.

My experience is that people who seek counselling to work on problems related to traumatic experiences tend to welcome the breath work component. However, breath work is not for everyone. Some individuals experience focusing on the breath as agitating, and therefore, these types of safety practices are not a fit for them.

For those who welcome the breath work, once they learn the basics of how to do it, they readily take it up in future sessions. Sessions quickly develop a natural rhythm that mixes "regular" talk therapy with that of the breath work type of therapeutic conversation.

In later meetings, some individuals expressly request constructive breath work and then proceed to use it during the entire conversation. This tends to happen after individuals have already sorted out some important understandings and have zeroed in on the particular themes about which they want further clarity.

These later sessions tend to be more about using the breath work to strengthen the understandings that the individual has already identified and elucidated. It is a way of thickening the plot, so to speak.

Regardless of the purpose of the breath work techniques, I endeavour to integrate them into a narrative framework as much as possible. In so doing, my intention is to provide tools for individuals to use to create safety, which in turn allows them to further develop their own sense of personal agency.

PARTICULARS OF THE BREATH WORK

When I introduce someone to the breath work, I acknowledge and make explicit that I am doing most of the talking and generating most of the ideas at this time, but that this is only for the purposes of demonstration. I explicitly set the expectation that I will eventually hand off much of this responsibility so that it is the individual who will be doing most of the talking and generating most of the content.

I also acknowledge that I'm utilizing the knowledge I've gained from others with whom I have previously worked. That is, I make the distinction that I offer ideas and suggestions that come from individuals with similar concerns. With restorative breath work, I share examples of different patterns of breathing that other individuals have found helpful. With constructive breath work, I share examples of worry counterstatements from previous individuals' work as a means of introducing the technique.

Using insider knowledge allows me to provide information in a somewhat more de-centred way. In other words, it is not just my expertise that I am offering up, but it is also the expertise of individuals who have knowledge and experience related to whatever we are currently working on. Rather than being squarely in the expert role of advisor, I strive to be in the more de-centred role of facilitator.

The breath work practices are also a kind of noticing task and introduce the idea of body awareness. As discussed in detail above, much of the discomfort in trauma work resides in the physiological experience that comes along with it. I believe that figuring out how to manage the body piece of the effects of trauma starts with an understanding of our bodies, learning how to notice and recognize the messages of our bodies, and then making sense of and responding to the signs of bodily tension, discomfort, and despair. Just as important, though often neglected, is being able to notice, recognize, make sense of, and respond to preferred bodily signs, such as a sense of calm, the experience of release, and feelings of joy.

I've found it is also helpful to do the breath work alongside the individual. My personal experience has shown me that my state of being impacts that of the individual with whom I am working.

Doing the breathing part of this work with the person helps me stay calm, grounded, and steady in the role of keeper of the safety. It also allows me to demonstrate the technique and enhances my connection with the individual.

PARTICULARS OF THE CONSTRUCTIVE BREATH WORK

When I initiate constructive breath work, I ensure the individual understands that they are not expected to come up with ideas right now but that I do hope they will use the "veto card" to change or reject any ideas I present. I let individuals know I want them to just say no to my ideas when something is not right for them. I welcome this kind of feedback. I find the more feedback and direction an individual gives me, the faster and more effective this part of the work is.

During the breath work practices, I step more intentionally into an externalizing conversation. (I describe externalizing conversations in more detail in Chapter 4. However, for a full discourse on the subject, please see Chapter 1 in Michael White's *Maps of Narrative Practice.*) I use the language of personal agency—the kind of language that allows individuals to separate themselves from the problem, analyze it, manipulate it, and gain mastery over it. It is a way for me to assist people in viewing a worry or any other concern as something that gets in the way of the therapeutic work rather than viewing it as an integral part of their identity.

I speak about the worries in an externalizing fashion, describing them as a *thing* that gets in the way of work, an *entity* that comes to mind, *something* to which one can respond. For example, I might say, "We will first identify a worry, idea, or even an image that you suspect is getting in the way of your work. Then we will look at that idea and create a preferred response to it that reduces or changes its hindering impact."

I avoid using words or phrases like "You are worried ..." or "your worries" or "your anxiety." This kind of language tends to locate the worry within the person or suggest it is a part of their personal identity. In contrast to externalizing language, these words and phrases often lead to a thin description of worry and tend to lend the worries a more intractable kind of quality.

I've also discovered how important it is to acknowledge the individual's own unique contribution of insider information. That is, when an individual generates a unique idea or understanding that they have found particularly helpful, I will often ask if I can share that idea with others.

I am constantly collecting the gold nuggets of wisdom from individuals who are working on challenging issues with my intention of sharing them with others in future sessions. These gold nuggets, or pieces of insider information, are of great value to me as a practitioner because they are tried-and-true suggestions and ideas. The fact that they have proven useful to one person means they will likely resonate with others.

In acknowledging the value of these ideas, I am affirming individuals as being the expert of their own lives and in the resolution of their own problems. Asking permission to share these understandings and insights with others who may be struggling with similar problems further helps to consolidate the value and utility of their initiatives.

Individuals are contributing to the well-being of others through the sharing of their brave work and supporting me in my work. There is a mutual connection of shared goals and of working together that can be quite powerful.

SIMPLICITY AND COMPLEXITY OF THE BREATH WORK

Incorporating the two kinds of breath work into the therapeutic conversation may seem like a fairly simple and straightforward activity. It is. And it isn't. This is what is simple and straightforwards about breath work:

- It is accessible to both the individual and the practitioner. All you need is your breath and your voice. As long as you are both able to breathe and speak, which hopefully is true during every session, you can do the breath work.
- It is possible to get results in a short time. With respect to restorative breath work, the 5-Minute Breathing Task is a testimony to this statement. Within five minutes, the person has been able to notice their own breathing rate, implement breathing techniques, and create a noticeable and desired change.

  The use of constructive breath work to address therapy worries also results in an experience of relief and calm that is achieved relatively quickly, often within the timespan of a single session, as was the case for Julia.
- Breath work is flexible and transportable. It can be done anytime and anywhere. Whether one is focusing on just breathing (restorative) or one is combining statements with intentional breathing (constructive), the breath work can be done in one's head.

- Its range of application is broad. Individuals with whom I have worked have found these techniques useful for a range of situations: sitting in the dentist's chair, being benched at a school basketball game, waiting in the office prior to a big meeting, riding the bus to school, or waiting to testify against a family member who has committed sexual assault.
- It does not require extensive formal training to learn how to do it. People with little to no training in breathing techniques can learn how to do restorative and constructive breath work within one or two therapy sessions. Outside of the therapy room, individuals can acquire knowledge and skills about breath work techniques relatively easily through a variety of sources (e.g., meditation and yoga classes).

This is what is *not* simple and straightforwards about breath work:

- It is tricky to use on oneself when working on highly distressing and complex problems. This is not surprising since more upsetting problems bring with them a greater intensity of emotional and physiological disruption.

  Intense emotion and high levels of agitation cloud the mind and agitate the body. This makes it challenging to settle into any kind of breath work technique. Additionally, intense emotion and agitation can interfere with the ability to focus on one's breathing and can interfere with the ability to find the words needed to create an impactful statement during constructive breath work.

Therefore, these types of problems are best reserved for times when a person can be with a skilled listener or counsellor who can facilitate the person's ability to focus on the breath and generate preferred counterstatements.

- It takes time to establish the habit of using this skill. Like any new skill, one must practice it enough to get comfortable with it and develop the discernment around when to use it.

  In the context of therapy, one must learn to discern when to take a break from the meaning-based therapeutic conversation to do the restorative work (e.g., the 5-Minute Breathing Task or a version thereof). With constructive breath work, which is embedded in the meaning-based therapeutic conversation, one must also learn to discern which understandings are breath work worthy.
- It takes time to learn how to craft statements with impact for constructive breath work. If the statements are either too generalized or too complicated, then the technique will be less effective and may even be ineffective. Learning how to craft sentiments that are just specific enough and at a manageable level of difficulty takes some time and practice. In essence, discernment with respect to the complexity of language and the degree of manageable change is key.
- Breath work involves integrating several types of skills. Though it looks like just breathing and speaking, any breathing technique involves utilizing several other skills and knowledges, such as body awareness, word knowledge (vocabulary), memory recall, auditory short-term memory, understanding of learning style, and overall discernment.

> Formal or informal training in body-mind disciplines (e.g., yoga and mindfulness) is very helpful. I received formal training in several body-mind techniques and informal training in others. I found all these learnings useful in helping me to hone the skill of using breath work in both my personal and professional life.

As safety techniques, I find the breath work tools to be a useful addition to the therapeutic process. This is particularly the case for the constructive, meaning-making type of breath work. That is, when a person uses the constructive breath work technique to address therapy worries, they are creating a scaffold for doing similar kinds of work for the later externalizing and re-authoring types of conversations. Individuals become more confident with the breath work practice as they move through the different stages of the work.

This growing confidence translates into the development of a greater sense of safety as the work progresses. Thus, by the time individuals approach the core trauma work—which involves the most sensitive and highly charged material—they are better able to navigate the therapeutic process in a safe and non-traumatizing manner.

THE SAFETY CHECK-IN

The safety check-in, like the breath work, is another tool I use to help bolster a sense of safety when working with trauma and tremendous hardship. Though not a breath work practice in and of itself, the safety check-in can be a useful accompaniment to the breath work.

It involves using a rating scale, which acts as a kind of informal assessment tool for gauging the safety in the room. In using rating scales, I am drawing on the Solution-Focused Brief Therapy work of Steve de Shazer[26] and others to aid in externalizing the problems that can get in the way of safety. The information gained from the scaling questions allows the individual and me to determine if any safety adjustments are needed.

The safety check-in is also an opportunity to use externalizing language—a manner of talking about the problem that encourages a sense of personal agency over the problem—which also promotes a sense of safety.

There are two parts to the safety check-in: the initial scaling exercise at the beginning of the session and another closing scaling exercise near the end of the session. The scale I use is the Solid/Shaky Scale, and it is used to rate the level of comfort or ease that the individual is experiencing. The scale is from 1 to 10, with a 10 indicating a high level of feeling solid and at ease and a 1 meaning a low level.

I create my scales with a built-in emphasis on those feeling states that are helpful and supportive of the work (e.g., feeling solid, comfortable, and at ease) over those feeling states that are disruptive to the work (e.g., anxiety, worry, nervousness, etc.). That is, the higher numbers represent a greater degree of the desirable feelings or qualities and lower numbers represent less of the desirable feelings.

In creating the scale this way, I am making two assumptions. One assumption is that working in a state of comfort and ease is

26 de Shazer, S. (1985). *Keys to solution in brief therapy*. W. W. Norton & Company.

safer than working in a state of discomfort and distress. The other is that the individual would prefer to work in a way that feels safer.

And so, I set up my scale with a bias towards those qualities that I believe the individual wants to enhance rather than those qualities that the individual wants to reduce. That way, the conversation becomes more about noticing comfort and ease and how to create more of it rather than just being about noticing discomfort and distress and how to create less of it. It is one small way to further develop safety.

Initial Safety Check-In

Sometimes, I introduce the initial safety check-in right at the beginning of the first session. However, more often I introduce it after I have outlined how I work using some version of the introductory therapy map.

Following is an example of how I might introduce the safety check-in and the Solid/Shaky Scale:

> *So, I mentioned to you the idea that this kind of work can be hard work but that it doesn't have to be hopeless, overwhelming, and despairing work. Again, this comes back to feeling safe from the pull of the pit of despair or the horror that is often connected to the experience of the trauma/abuse/hardship.*
>
> *Sometimes this kind of work brings with it Anxiety, Stress, and Worry, which can make doing the work feel unsafe or scary. One of the things I like to use to help us keep on the safe and hopeful track is a check-in. Are you okay to give that a whirl right now?*

[The individual verbally agrees.]

An easy and concrete way to do a check-in is for us to use a scale that measures your level of comfort. I also call this the Solid versus Shaky Scale. The scale ranges from 1 to 10, with a 1 meaning you are feeling a low level of "Solidness" (and a high level of "Shakiness") and a 10 meaning you are feeling a high level of "Solidness" (and a low level of "Shakiness").

Shakiness could also show up in the form of Anxiety, Stress, Worry, Nervousness, or whatever "feeling shaky" means for you. For example, you might rate yourself as a 1 because you are experiencing a lot of Nervousness or Agitation. A rating of 5 on this scale would mean things are at a middling level for you; perhaps there is a fairly even mix of different types of feelings (e.g., Nervousness pairing up with Confidence) resulting in feeling a medium level of Ease and Solidness.

A rating of 10 means that you are experiencing a strong feeling of Solidness. Feeling solid could also show up as Confidence, Ease, Comfort, Calm, Steadiness, or whatever "feeling solid" means for you.

So, where do you figure your comfort level is right now based on this scale? And, by the way, it can be a best guess or a range; it doesn't have to be too precise.

[Individual states a number or range of numbers.]

Okay, great, thanks. Could you just write that number down? We will do some work together and then check in again before you leave, okay?

I find drawing out the scale—having a visual representation—is much more effective than just speaking about the scale. I like to use bar graphs and line graphs. I prefer handwritten, in-the-moment depictions to formal, prefabricated, and expert-looking diagrams.

These types of scribbled diagrams, when embedded in a de-centred but influential approach, are a means by which we can work together to create the scale that best fits the person at that moment in that particular session. They are collaborative tools. And they are simple and user-friendly:

FIGURE 1: Solid/Shaky Scale

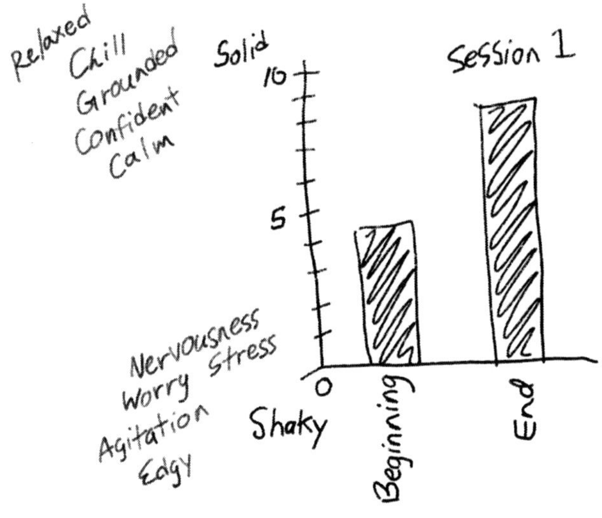

I set up my check-in scales using externalizing language. Rather than saying "Your Worry/Anxiety can get in the way of doing the work today, yes?" to talk about the problematic feeling states, I say something like "Worry and Anxiety have a way of getting in the way of work. Is this happening for you?" Or I ask, "Are Worry and Anxiety showing up for you and making it more difficult for you to do this work?"

Once the individual has identified which feeling states are running interference, we can then assess how they might be affecting their level of ease and comfort by implementing the scale. Again, using externalizing language, I ask something like "Right now, on a scale of 1 to 10, what level of 'feeling solid' are you at? How strong is a Sense of Calm/Groundedness/Ease right now?" Putting feeling states in this kind of externalizing language allows the individual to analyze them and measure them more easily.

In setting up rating scales, I seek to discover from the individual their preferred way of describing the feeling states. However, because this work of self-reflection and problem-solving requires a great deal of mental energy, I am interested in making this task as effortless as possible. To this end, I provide a range of word choices and ask which ones, if any, resonate. This is a way to scaffold the task and still privilege the person's word(s) over mine. I do this verbally and visually. That is, as I talk, I also write down lists of words for them to consider.

Like the offering of word choices, the use of two modes of presentation allows the person to complete the task more quickly and with less mental effort. Individuals often will choose a particular word that resonates most with them; frequently, they will come up with their own descriptor.

Closing Safety Check-In

About two-thirds of the way through the session, I check in again with the person using the same rating scale. I have found it is helpful to introduce the closing safety check-in in a way that allows enough time to address the possibility of a low score on the Solid/Shaky Scale. This is more important in the early stages of therapy. Over time, the individual gains mastery over managing anxiety and worry, and so less time is required for them to address low scores on the scale.

Often individuals are feeling a noticeable sense of relief and renewed hope at the conclusion of the first meeting. When I ask them to rate how they feel on the Solid/Shaky Scale, most people report numbers between 7 and 10, indicating high levels of calm/comfort or feeling solid.

However, on a few occasions, the opposite is true and the individual is feeling overwhelmed. For example, this can happen when a person brings up particularly painful memories towards the end of our time together. If this occurs and the person's rating is below a 5, I ask, "What is the lowest number at which you feel you would be good to go?" or "What number is high enough for you to feel okay leaving the session and still able to manage your day-to-day life?"

If the person's current number is lower than their preferred end-of-session number, I ask them if they would like to do a bit of grounding breath work to raise the rating up to the desired level. At this point in our work together, the individual has already been introduced to the breath work; this is now an opportunity to practice it. Working together, we craft grounding statements and then pair them with breath work.

This is another occasion where the pendulum swings me more towards the centred end of the relationship. But I believe I must step into a more centred role because the individual has indicated an unacceptable level of vulnerability, and this speaks to a lack of safety. I see this as a sign for me, the therapist, to step up with regard to the role of keeper of the safety and to be more directive. Again, I strive to make this shift as collaborative as possible and with an eye for moving back towards a more de-centred position as soon as possible.

Often the kinds of statements that help people find their sense of grounding at the end of a session can be the ones that they created earlier to address their therapy worries. For example, the following statements often warrant repeating in this situation:

1. I need to keep in mind that I don't have to fix everything right now. <breath>
2. I can give myself credit for making it to this meeting and see that as a step in the right direction. <breath>
3. I can be open to allowing myself the time and space I need to move forwards in my work with regard to Problem X. <breath>

If these statements are not enough for the person, then I ask about the kinds of things they typically do to make themselves feel better when they are upset. I also ask about who they have in their life that is supportive. Then, I offer some grounding statements that incorporate these personal resources. For example:

1 I can figure out how to get my level of calm up to a 5 [or whatever is the individual's preferred level for being able to manage the rest of the day]. <breath>
2 I can take some time right now to figure out how to raise my level of calm to a 5. <breath>
3 I know I can get myself more grounded, calm, and relaxed by listening to music [or whatever activity helps the individual feel calmer]. <breath> And I can bring that knowledge forwards to help me get grounded right now. <breath>
4 I know I can make myself feel better and stronger by going for a walk, hanging out with my friend, calling my auntie, texting my brother [or whatever activity helps the individual feel stronger]. <breath> And I can make those past experiences and the knowledge they bring available to me now. <breath>

I will then invite the individual to jot down those phrases or words that are most helpful to take away and use to facilitate calm and ease in their day-to-day life.

The safety check-in at the end of the session is useful for ensuring that the individual does not leave the therapy session feeling demoralized or vulnerable but rather leaves with a sense of renewed hope and purpose. It functions as a kind of brief, informal risk assessment.

This helps the person keep the hard work of healing from trauma in a place that is manageable and hopeful. It is a practice that supports the individual to sustain the work of healing outside the therapy session.

The Usefulness of the Safety Check-In

It was the use of the safety check-in that demonstrated to me just how big a deal it is for most people to come to therapy for any kind of work, not just trauma therapy. Cognitively, I understood that therapy is unnerving work for people, but for some reason, I was under the misguided impression that just getting to therapy would invariably result in a great sense of relief or a feeling of accomplishment for the person. Apparently not.

I am interested in better understanding and appreciating the incredibly challenging task of showing up to therapy to work on the serious issues of trauma and hardship. There is something very striking about a person sitting opposite you saying they are feeling like a 1, 2, or 3 out of a possible 10 in terms of comfort and ease. This is not just hard work; it is *really* hard work, and more than that, it is often very scary work.

For me, respecting and honouring this challenge is such an important part of the safety work. Doing the scaling exercise is a way of making the enormity of this undertaking more concrete for both the individual and for me. I have been gratified to learn that people are interested in doing these scales and are able to quickly and easily rate their level of comfort/discomfort.

Discovering the pervasiveness of this first-session unease (i.e., therapy worries) is what lead me to the conclusion that it makes sense to address it directly before diving into the primary therapeutic conversation. I was surprised by how low people rated themselves in that initial check-in; their ratings were usually between a 1 and a 4.

This reinforced for me the idea that most people were showing up not just with the problem stress but also with a cartload of worry about the therapy process itself. People's feelings of anxiety around doing the counselling were very front and centre for them, and the intensity of these feelings was strong enough to impede their work on whatever problem or concern they had come to address. I developed this practice piece—the safety check-in followed by breath work—as a response to this initial state of unease.

Over the course of time, the safety check-in has become an important safety practice piece for me when working with individuals who are dealing with the effects of trauma. In fact, I use it throughout therapy because the unnerving effects of trauma can resurface at any time and bring with them disruptive feelings of agitation.

Using the Solid/Shaky Scale regularly, even in an abbreviated form, helps both the individual and me to keep our finger on the pulse of safety throughout the entire therapeutic process. In turn, this allows us to shore up the safety side of things before proceeding with riskier kinds of work (i.e., more emotionally charged issues).

AN EXAMPLE OF THE SAFETY CHECK-IN WITH CHEYENNE

My initial meeting with Cheyenne illustrates some of the useful—and sometimes unexpected—understandings that can be uncovered during a safety check-in. In particular, it highlights the kind of vulnerability factors that can influence a person's sense of safety in the therapy session.

Cheyenne's reason for meeting with me was because she was struggling with the effects of familial child sexual abuse. Obviously, this kind of serious violation with its accompanying severe abuse of power immediately raises concerns about a person's vulnerability.

In addition, there were several differences between Cheyenne and me that came into play with regard to her potential vulnerability: youth versus adult, minority (indigenous) versus dominant (white) culture, student versus staff. Never had I relied more upon the wisdom of the de-centred but influential position than in this particular therapeutic circumstance.

For me, what this meant was that I must take extra care to be transparent about the fact that I am not an expert on her experience, whether that be in the adolescent, cultural, or student context. Instead, I sought to convey that what I could offer her was help in discovering ideas about standing up to the effects of childhood sexual abuse.

Further, the understanding of our work together was that her lived experience of her own world(s) would guide us as we explored these ideas. I asked Cheyenne to correct and redirect me should I venture into territory that was not right for her.

I was pleasantly surprised by how quickly Cheyenne took me up on this request. She came across as gentle-spirited and soft-spoken, yet she was strong in her convictions. She did not hesitate to express to me when I had misunderstood her or was heading in a different direction than the one she wanted. She was clear, patient, and methodical.

We spent some of this first session sussing each other out. I shared with her a bit about how I worked. When I asked her about her hopes for our work together, she shared that she wanted to be able to better manage her inner turmoil. I experienced a wee twinge of surprise. To me, Cheyenne exuded such serenity and calm. In fact, I would say she appeared to me to be a very self-possessed and tranquil person.

Yet here she was in her gentle, quiet, precise way detailing to me the chaos and intensity of her inner world. She wanted some ways to manage the powerful emotions she was experiencing—sadness, anger, and irritation—so that she could better focus on her academics. Cheyenne identified this inner distress as a consequence of the abuse she had experienced, and she saw meeting with me as one way for her to stand up to it.

I introduced Cheyenne to the idea of using breath work. I suggested that we could use breath work on its own to calm the physical part of the emotional distress, or we could combine the breath work with thoughts and ideas and address those that were feeding the distressing emotions. Cheyenne was interested in exploring both options, and this is what we did.

After doing some of this work together, Cheyenne appeared to me to be feeling much more at ease. However, given my earlier misread, I made a mental note to make sure that I checked in with her at the end of our meeting.

As the time available to us was coming to an end, I initiated a check-in with her. To my dismay, I realized that I had neglected to introduce the safety check-in and the Solid/Shaky Scale at the beginning of our meeting. The more vulnerability factors in an individual's situation, the more I worry about their sense of safety being compromised, and therefore, the more critical it is for me to keep an eye on safety levels. Cheyenne's situation certainly qualified her as someone with the potential to be highly vulnerable. I needed to bring in the Solid/Shaky Scale:

"Cheyenne, usually when I meet with people who are working on serious concerns such as the ones you have mentioned, I do a little check-in thing using a rating scale. It has to do with seeing how you are doing at the end of our time together and to make sure that you are feeling okay enough to go about your day. Would you be okay doing this little exercise with me?"

"Sure."

"So how it works is the scale goes from 1 to 10. Ten means your level of feeling solid, grounded, relaxed, confident, and basically A-OK is high and shakiness is low. One means your level of comfort is low or the feeling of being shaky or agitated is high. A rating of 5 is somewhere in-between."

I quickly sketched out a line diagram of this scale as I described it:

"Approximately how would you rate your feelings right now on this scale? What number would you give them?"

Without hesitation, Cheyenne answered, "Oh, about a 4."

"A 4?" I inquired.

In my head, I was thinking "A 4?! What?! She is only at a 4? How could this be?" My curiosity was piqued. I really felt with all my therapist intuition that this session had gone much better than I'd expected. Regardless of how Cheyenne appeared to me, she had done what I thought was some remarkable work in a short time. She had effectively learned and used breath work to generate several meaningful statements.

Based on her level of engagement, focus, and concentration and the ideas she had explored, I concluded that Cheyenne had made some profound connections. I believed that she surely had moved to a much better place than when we first sat down together. So, how could her comfort level be sitting only at a 4?

While silently practicing my own therapist self-soothing statements in my head and taking a deep, slow breath, I said:

> *"Well, tell me, Cheyenne, I am wondering what a 4 means to you. Can you tell me a bit more about how you're feeling or what you're thinking about at this 4 level?"*
>
> *"Sure. It's good. It's fine," she replied. She was clear and matter of fact.*

I took another deep, cleansing breath and asked:

> *"So, it's fine? Do you think as you currently sit—at a 4—that you are able to go out of this office and manage your day-to-day life okay? Is it that kind of fine?"*
>
> *"Yep."*

At this point, I was quite curious and a bit bewildered because most individuals to whom I have asked this end-of-session rating question typically rate their level of calm or solidness at a 7 or more.

From what Cheyenne had said, she was good to go, and she did not need to do any more work with me that day. Yet her rating was below the halfway mark. As I was still concerned for her, I persisted:

"So usually, I ask people to do the rating scale at the beginning of our appointment. Then, we do some work, and I ask them again at the end. That's to make sure that the work we did together didn't create more distress. Sometimes that can happen when people are working on tough things.

I forgot to ask you at the beginning, so if it's okay with you, I'd like you to think back to when you first knocked on my door and sat down. Rewind the video, so to speak, and tell me what number you were at on this same scale when you first came in the room to see me."

"Maybe a 2 or a 1," Cheyenne answered quickly; it did not seem to be a difficult question for her.

"Okay, so is the shakiness/distress lower now than when you first came in? You are feeling more solid?"

"Yes."

"Just out of curiosity, what's your best guess at your usual or average level on this scale? You know, like, over the course of the week, what level of solid versus shaky are you at most of the time or most often? What's your usual day-to-day operating level?"

"Probably a 2."

"Okay. So, most of the time you are feeling pretty shaky?"

She nodded.

"And what's the highest number of solidness or confidence that you think you have been at over the last little while?"

"Probably about a 4."

"Similar to how you feel right now?"

"Yep."

Now it was dawning on me what the numbers meant to her and how that was different from my understanding. Here was a young person who outwardly showed herself to be managing things. However, inwardly, she often was experiencing intense distress. And this distress was something that had been around for a long time.

Thus, on Cheyenne's scale of what was reasonable (or perhaps even possible) for her right now, the highest number was only around a 4. She could not even recall a time when she felt higher levels of confidence, calm, or ease. Now her responses made perfect sense to me. Now I was ready to ask the final check-in question of this exercise:

"Cheyenne, at this 4 level, do you feel good to go? That you can manage your everyday life? That you will be okay?"

"Oh yeah, no problem. I am good to go."

Concluding Thoughts

The de-centred but influential relationship is the foundation upon which all safety practices are built. Therefore, it is important to establish this relational foundation before introducing the safety practices. I am harkening back yet again to the importance of the therapeutic alliance.

However, as a practitioner, I find it is so easy to get caught up in the excitement of sharing interventions and techniques and veer too much into being-the-expert territory. This diminishes the individual's voice and can compromise their sense of personal agency, both of which are inextricably intertwined with feeling safe.

In an effort to resist the pull of this temptation, I have installed an alert system in the therapy-best-practices part of my brain that goes off intermittently and repeats the following mantras: Relationship is top dog. Relationship trumps tools or methods or techniques. That means any ideas or tools that I provide, such as the breath work techniques and the safety check-in, are useful only as long as they are in service to the relationship, not the other way around. Focus on relationship as the first order of safety. Then focus on safety tools.

I rely more heavily on this self-monitoring system when I am introducing safety tools because, by necessity, this work must be driven by therapist knowledge and expertise. Although I constantly evaluate how I can impart these safety pieces in a manner that is as de-centred as possible, I traverse deeper into therapist-centred territory to convey these safety practices. Then,

I retreat back to a more de-centred position to support the individual with reconstructing their understandings.

My primary justification for straying away from the de-centred but influential position at all is that I believe the physical component of safety in this work is so critical. These safety tools are a means of giving the body a voice. In so doing, the body becomes a full participant and is given agency in the therapeutic conversation and the subsequent re-authoring of the trauma experience.

In other words, I am making the case that there is a time and a place for the practitioner to step into a more centred domain, and that time occurs primarily during the introduction of safety tools. However, I am also making the case for doing so in a circumscribed manner with the intention of stepping back into more de-centred territory as quickly as possible.

As individuals move through the stages of trauma work, they will continue to cultivate and further develop their safety practices securely within the protective context of the de-centred but influential relationship. Regardless of the therapeutic work at hand, the individuals are better able to address the safety issues in an emergent and confident manner. This amalgamation of therapeutic process variables is key for supporting a safe, non-traumatizing resolution of the trauma experience.

CHAPTER 3

Safety Tools for the Practitioner

REBECCA GREETED ME with a friendly hello and a warm yet restrained smile. I welcomed her into my office. I offered her a seat and a glass of water.

This was not Rebecca's first meeting with me. Originally, she'd met with me to seek help for the intense anxiety that her 5-year-old daughter, Alyssa, was experiencing. Alyssa would become fraught with anxiety when she was separated from her mother. This had become particularly troublesome when it was time for Alyssa to begin attending kindergarten. Anxiety showed up for Alyssa in the form of worry thoughts about something catastrophic happening to her mother.

Over the course of that mother-daughter work, I had witnessed Rebecca's conscientious, thoughtful, and loving exchanges with her daughter as they worked together to put Alyssa's worry thoughts in their place. During this time, Rebecca uncovered an important connection between her daughter's reluctance to go off to school and her own past traumatic experiences. Rebecca determined that one of the effects of the trauma was its influence on her relationship with her daughter. She believed that it had contributed to the development of a protective but anxious connection.

Now, we were meeting again to begin her own work. She was determined to deal with the effects of past trauma that were still impacting her relationship with her daughter. Absent for the moment was the calm, gentle, supportive mother of previous sessions. Rebecca's demeanour had shifted to a different place. Before me sat a nervous, tentative woman. We exchanged some pleasantries, and then we turned our energy and focus to our work together.

Rebecca began with a kind of confession. She told me that she knows she should have worked on these issues long ago but was afraid to go to counselling. The reason for her fear stemmed from something a friend had shared with her. This friend, like her, had witnessed horrific atrocities when he was living in a war-torn nation. Like her, he was haunted by the effects of what he had witnessed.

As she continued to relate this story, Rebecca's voice became tremulous. In a whisper, she spoke of her friend who had found the courage to seek help and meet with a counsellor. The counsellor had become so unsettled after listening to his story that she had abruptly terminated their work; it had ended before it had barely begun. The counsellor told her friend that she found it too distressing to work with him after hearing his story. He was devastated by this and warned Rebecca about this potential hazard. Rebecca, in turn, was deeply affected by her friend's experience; she could not face counselling. It was many years later that she was able to muster up the courage to give counselling a chance.

"This is a game-changer." Julia looked at me with intensity and repeated the sentiment. "This is a game-changer." She was emphatic that I understood how big this was for her. She had just concluded some intense work—what I refer to as core trauma work. "I just was able to describe what happened to me as an

8-year-old girl in detail, and it was okay. This is so different from that other counselling session where I felt dirty and re-violated."

Julia went on to elaborate the differences. She told me how, over the course of several decades, she had seen several counsellors in her efforts to heal from the effects of childhood sexual abuse. Julia had found many of these professionals to be helpful. However, she told me that one of her strongest memories of therapy was a disturbing one:

> *This happened early on in my life. It was one of my first therapists, and she wanted me to re-tell my sexual abuse incidents starting immediately with our second visit–*yikes! *Was that ever disturbing and seemed so inappropriate! She had no idea how intense, severe, and frequent my sexual abuse had been.*
>
> *It was like* [the therapist] *wanted the nitty-gritty, play-by-play of the events. It had kind of a voyeuristic feel to it. To this day, 30 years later, I still do not understand the purpose of that exercise, and suffice it to say, I never returned to see her.*

Julia concluded that the therapist's response had created a distressing lack of safety in the therapy session.

Practitioner Response and the Risk of Re-traumatization

The 30-something mother of a school-aged child and the 50-something mother of adult children: two individuals with different backgrounds, at different stages of life, and with distinct experiences of trauma, but both articulated a common disturbing theme. They both shared a profound experience of alienation directly linked to the influence of the "helping" professional.

These examples illustrate how re-traumatization can occur as a consequence of the practitioner's response. It is this risk that I wish to address here.

I do not know the prevalence of re-traumatization as a result of professional intervention. What I do know from my own work is that even these few instances were troubling enough to spur me on to develop more elaborate safety practices.

In my efforts to avoid this therapy pitfall as much as possible, I have found it useful to create a regimen of preventive safety measures. Given the centrality of the therapeutic relationship, it makes sense that safety practices revolve around the development of a sound and safe therapeutic alliance. Cultivating a de-centred but influential position with the individual is one way of achieving this. Cultivating a solid, grounded, and steady practitioner presence is another way.

The former focuses on the practitioner skills of being carefully attuned to the individual. The latter focuses on the practitioner skills of being carefully attuned to themselves. As a practitioner, if I am to be mindful of my influence and manage it effectively, I believe I must understand in depth what that influence looks, feels, and sounds like.

One way that I strive to foster this self-understanding is by identifying and working with whatever personal issues I have that could get in the way of my ability to be fully present and attuned to the individual. What are my areas of vulnerability? How do I prepare for the unwelcome appearance of my own vulnerabilities in the therapy session? Addressing practitioner vulnerabilities supports practitioner self-care and skill development while simultaneously contributing to the creation of a safe therapeutic relationship.

It seems to me that in more recent times, practitioners are focusing more on their own personal well-being and how that influences their work. Practitioner self-care (and I would include practitioner self-awareness within this domain) continues to gain traction in the helping professions; I see the rise of mindfulness concepts in the mental health field as one example of this trend. In this chapter, I add my voice to this initiative.

Practitioner Vulnerabilities and Self-Care in Trauma Therapy

It is probably safe to say that each of us has vulnerabilities and weaknesses unique to our own particular learning, experience, and biology. I also acknowledge that all practitioners are constantly working on developing healthy practices with respect to the creation of an effective therapeutic alliance. That is what we do. Establishing a regular, preventive routine to ensure that we as counsellors deal with personal vulnerabilities on an emergent basis can enhance the efficacy of our practice.

In the context of trauma therapy, however, I have found additional practices are helpful for supporting a safe therapeutic environment. Again, this goes back to that inherent quality of trauma work: the requirement of working with highly charged, emotional material. There is an intensity to trauma work that is not necessarily present in other types of counselling. This intensity operates across domains: cognitive, emotional, and physical.

The potency of the physiological component is the piece that makes trauma work especially tricky. A practitioner's physiology is influenced by the physiology of the individual with whom they are working and vice versa. Being mentally and physiologically strong allows the practitioner to better navigate whatever transpires in the therapeutic relationship.

I think of this ability to be mentally and physiologically strong and steady as being grounded. The grounded therapist is someone who is better equipped to create and sustain a safe and secure territory in which the individual's work can unfold.

My conclusion is that trauma work requires extra precautions with respect to how we safeguard the attunement aspect of the therapeutic relationship. We need to be especially meticulous about how we show up in therapy to ensure that the relationship remains in service to the individual.

To that end, I have found it helpful to formalize and make self-care practices part of my routine. Here, I offer what I have found useful in the hope that it is helpful to others who wish to enhance or refresh their own particular safety regimen. These practices range from general self-care practices to those that are specific to a particular therapy session.

Practices for Self-Care

Habits of general self-care make a person stronger, healthier, and more able to be effective in one's work. Though this statement may be self-evident, I find knowing it is much easier than actually living it. There are a myriad of healthy habits that support us to function better regardless of our chosen vocation. Diet and nutrition, physical fitness, work-life balance, interpersonal relationships, and other aspects of life all have an influence on our overall performance as human beings. It is useful to attend to these in general.

But beyond these basics, I have found certain self-care practices—both personal ones and therapy-based ones—are especially helpful for me when working with trauma. These practices cultivate a sense of clarity and calm, which in turn allow me to hone self-awareness. Those qualities help me to be a more grounded practitioner.

PERSONAL SELF-CARE PRACTICES

The personal self-care practices that I want to highlight are those that, in addition to being personally beneficial, also teach skills that are most salient to maintaining a grounded presence in the therapy context. The habits I rely most heavily on include:

- Breath work
- Meditation
- Morning pages
- Yoga
- Cranial sacral therapy

I initiated most of these self-care methods as a means of rehabilitating the physical injuries I sustained when I played competitive sports. However, I quickly realized that they offer much more than the remediation of bodily harm. Now, I rely on them primarily for supporting my mental health and for developing my understanding of mindfulness and body-mind connections. Body-mind awareness has become an increasingly important component of the trauma work that I do. Sustaining and developing my own set of mindfulness practices serves a dual purpose: it provides self-care for me so that I can work more effectively, and it also informs my therapeutic practice.

Breath Work

The two main types of breath work tools that I use for my own self-care—restorative and constructive—are those that I originally developed as safety supports for individuals working with me on the effects of trauma (see Chapter 2).

RESTORATIVE BREATH WORK

The 5-Minute Breathing Task is a tool I developed to help others quickly and easily interrupt an emotional escalation and calm both body and mind. In my personal life, I mainly use this task as a preparation for meditation or as a quick body-mind reset when I have suddenly lost my attention or self-composure. In my work life, I may use it to prepare myself before a session.

CONSTRUCTIVE BREATH WORK

Constructive breath work is more involved than restorative as it uses breath work to help construct new, preferred meanings for oneself. With respect to my own self-care, I discovered that constructive breath work enables me to be much more successful with other self-soothing techniques.

For example, for most of my life I suffered from insomnia. Getting to sleep was difficult for me, because my brain seemed to think that bedtime was the perfect time to ramp up and sort out all my issues. Usually worries took up most of my brain's attention, but I also found my thoughts moving to other realms: planning my day, week, or life; my children's activities; work projects; etc.

I would try various pre-sleep techniques such as creating restful routines; doing relaxation exercises; visualizing my safe, quiet happy place; and/or deep breathing—all to no avail. I usually ended up exasperated and more alert due to the relentless and intrusive antics of my busy mind. I just could not seem to still the circles of thought that were spinning in my head. I would eradicate one stream of thought, and sure enough, another 1 or 2 or 10 different streams would just pop up into my consciousness.

Eventually, I discovered that if I did a constructive breath work exercise first and addressed my most intrusive thoughts directly, I could then make the relaxation exercises work. This led me to create sleep statements (see Appendix C). It was at this point that I learned how to fall asleep quickly and easily.

The idea that scaffolded this new understanding for me was this: sometimes the potency of distracting thoughts needed to be addressed first. And when I say addressed, I mean these thoughts had to be reworked, quietened, or subdued somehow—not just ignored or put aside—before I could be successful with certain self-soothing or mindfulness practices.

Meditation

My original purpose for learning about meditation was to help me better manage the day-to-day stress and demands of the three cherished roles in my life—wife, mother, and counsellor. I turned to mindfulness meditation as a starting point for developing a formal personal practice.

As I gained more experience and training in mindfulness, I was impressed by the scope of potential benefits for myself. This led me to explore its therapeutic value for my work. Only in the past five years or so have I attained a measure of consistency with regard to sustaining a daily personal practice. It took considerable time and effort for me to get to this point.

This was partly due to my particular learning style, which could be described as a tendency towards divergent thinking (taking ideas in many different directions), a preference for simultaneous processing (details held together by the big picture and general themes) rather than sequential processing (specific details, one following after another), a sensitivity to sensory-motor input (highly attuned to visual, auditory, and tactile input), very quick processing speed, and a preference for kinesthetic learning (physical movement helps to consolidate information). Add to this mix a dash of distractibility, and needless to say, many of the skills associated with mindfulness meditation—sitting still, slowing the body and mind, and focusing on a single thing—were counterintuitive to me and initially presented me with a formidable challenge.

I describe my struggles with acquiring this skill because I find that many of us who live in this fast-paced, technological Western world also experience similar challenges when it comes to mindfulness techniques. This is true even for individuals such as myself who have the added benefit of easy access to the skills and knowledge required for mindfulness.

At first glance, it seems like mindfulness meditation would be an easy skill to acquire. After all, it just requires being able to breathe and to pay attention to one's own thoughts. It seems like a no-brainer, so to speak. Wrong. For many of us, myself included, acquiring the skill of mindfulness can be a journey fraught with frustration and a sense of failure. It can be uncomfortable, arduous, and slow to learn. Those wonderful benefits can be difficult to attain and hard to sustain.

Ironically, the very reason behind this difficulty is often the same reason we seek to acquire these skills in the first place: our minds are agitated, overexcited, too rushed, too full, and too distracted. This frenzied state of mind not only interferes with efficiency in thinking, but it also impinges on our sense of well-being. Like the caged hamster on its wheel, our minds never seem able to catch up. Whether due to learning style, attention problems, emotional upheaval such as anxiety, or just plain busyness, many of our minds are often in or on the brink of overwhelm.

It appears to me that this predicament is related to one of the dominant discourses of our Western world, the thesis of which is higher, faster, busier, and more is better. Our minds respond to these ongoing demands by becoming busier and busier. When our minds operate so often in high gear, we can end up shifting into overdrive or, conversely, even into shut-down mode. The possible effects of all this include restlessness, agitation, worry, anxiety, insomnia, and exhaustion, to name a few.

A turning point in my learning curve was when I took a six-week online course on mindfulness meditation.[27] This course

---

27 Mindful Schools. (n.d.). 101: *Mindfulness foundations*. https://www.mindfulschools.org/training/101-mindfulness-foundations/

gave me the structure I needed to really embrace mindfulness meditation. It provided me with the big picture understanding of meditation and a range of interesting (i.e., divergent) learnings. Most importantly, it taught me the requisite skills in very small incremental steps.

When I began the course, getting through a three-minute meditation was challenging but doable. By the end of the course, a 30-minute meditation was a beautiful (and attainable) thing. It was at this point that I began to fully realize the benefits of a regular practice.

Though initially difficult to establish, I now have a set of daily mindfulness practices that are useful tools for helping me grow a sense of physical calm and clarity of mind in both my personal and professional life. Most mornings, I can drop into a 10-minute meditation and feel like it has helped set my mind on a clear path for the day. Other times, I may need more structure first before settling into meditation; if so, I will use constructive breath work to clear out a few supercharged thought patterns, or I will do the 5-Minute Breathing Task.

I now have a range of favourite meditations that I like to use. (See Resources at the end of the book.) When I am looking for clarity, focus, and calmness of mind, I tend to turn to mindfulness meditation. When I am looking for more spiritual calm or a sense of deep relaxation or peace, I turn to mantra-based practices or yoga nidra.

Clarity and a sense of calm are the two most obvious benefits of meditation. However, for me, the most important learning of meditation is the knowledge that I can be in charge of my own state of being. Regardless of the chaos in my life (or in a session), meditation has taught me that I have the ability to find clarity and calm in my mind and body. The development of this skill has been significant to me as a person; incorporating this skill into my work has been invaluable to me as a practitioner.

Morning Pages

I started this mindfulness activity as a tool to support the creative process for my writing. The morning pages is the primary tool developed by Julia Cameron for what she calls creative recovery: "Simply put, the morning pages are three pages of longhand writing, strictly stream-of-consciousness."[28] This tool is for anyone who wants to improve their creativity and output, regardless of the nature of their work; it is not just meant for writers.

I find that the writing process removes the flotsam and jetsam from my often overtired and busy mind by putting it on the page. For me, it has evolved into a regular daily practice that, like my morning meditation, serves the purpose of creating clarity and calmness for the mind.

Yoga

My fascination with yoga began in my 20s when I used it to stretch my overworked and aching muscles. Initially, I appreciated its benefits on a purely physical level: more flexibility, balance, and core strength. Now in my 50s, the aspects I relish the most are those that focus on emotional well-being and balance.

The yogic breath techniques teach not only how to breathe in general but also how to breathe for a specific purpose. The body

28 Cameron, J. (1992). *The artist's way: A spiritual path to higher creativity*. Penguin Putnam, Inc. p. 73.

awareness techniques of yoga include how to scan the body for areas of tension and how to use the breath as a tool for releasing the tension. These practices have proven very useful with respect to cultivating a sense of groundedness in both my personal and professional life.

Cranial Sacral Therapy

Cranial sacral therapy (CST), which is practiced mainly by massage therapists and physiotherapists, falls under the umbrella of alternative health treatments. CST is a philosophy of treatment that uses gentle touch to help turn down the body's stress response, and this allows the nervous system to facilitate self-correction. More specifically:

> CranioSacral Therapy (CST) is a gentle, hands-on method of evaluating and enhancing the functioning of a physiological body system called the cranial sacral system—comprised of membranes and cerebrospinal fluid that surround and protect the brain and spinal cord. Using a soft touch generally no greater than five grams, or about the weight of a nickel, practitioners release restrictions in the craniosacral system, which has been shown to improve the functioning of the central nervous system, as well as many other systems of the body, such as digestive, musculoskeletal, respiratory, circulatory, and more.[29]

29 Upledger Institute International. (n.d.) *Discover craniosacral therapy and somato-emotional release.* https://www.upledger.com/therapies/

I discovered CST in my search for relief from activity-related injuries. Similar to yoga, I found the technique offered more than injury rehabilitation. It soothes the central nervous system, which produces a sense of calm in the body and clarity of the mind. I have found it to be yet another useful body-mind tool in that it teaches me about patterns of holding tension in the body and how to release them.

THERAPY-BASED SELF-CARE PRACTICES

The personal self-care practices allowed me to gain a greater sense of calm, clarity of mind, and sense of groundedness, all qualities that helped me to better navigate my personal life. It made sense to me to apply some of these practices in a more intentional way to allow me to better navigate my work life.

As a practitioner, bringing a sense of calm, clarity of mind, and a sense of groundedness to the session allows me to be more effective in general, but in particular, it allows me to better create and sustain a sense of safety for the individual. For example, being grounded makes it easier to unearth any of my own unfinished personal business and prevent it from intruding upon the therapy process.

As well, these practices allow me to recover from any kind of disruption more quickly and efficiently. For example, when things feel like they are going terribly wrong in a session—like when the horror and despair of trauma gain unwanted entry into and power over the therapeutic conversation—these practices allow me to sustain a grounded presence, so I can more easily regain the calm and clarity I need to work effectively.

Two of the therapy-based self-care practices I use address therapy safety issues outside of the session. They involve anticipating and responding to any potential safety concerns and generating ideas for managing those concerns. They are the kinds of practices that most, if not all, counsellors do as a matter of course. I am highlighting them here as I believe they are especially important to utilize for cultivating safety when working with trauma. These are:

- Informal self-assessment of vulnerability
- Clinical consultation

Other practices support the creation of safety for a particular therapy session, and I use them at or around the time of the session. That is, I use them right before a session to prepare myself, during a session to aid in sustaining safety, or right after the conclusion of a session to discern whether or not any safety concerns have arisen that warrant extra follow-up. These types of self-care practices include:

- Review of session notes
- Body scan
- Constructive breath work

Sometimes these practices take a few minutes or, in the case of body scans, mere seconds. At other times, they require more time and energy to complete; this varies from session to session and from individual to individual.

All of these practices serve a similar function as the safety tools described in Chapter 2 in that their purpose is to enhance a sense of safety for the individual who is navigating the challenging work that is trauma therapy. The only difference is the focus—these practices focus on the practitioner whereas the safety tools described previously focus on the individual who is doing the trauma work. However, both sets of practices are geared towards cultivating a grounded and calm context for therapy.

Practices Used Outside of Sessions

INFORMAL SELF-ASSESSMENT OF VULNERABILITY

I recognize that the influence of certain challenges and hardships I have experienced in my life could overflow into my work in ways that are not useful to the person with whom I am working. To address this, I endeavour to raise my awareness of this potential hazard by reviewing my own history of hardship and challenge and focusing on those experiences that were most stressful and have the most emotional charge.

I find it is these emotionally charged experiences that make me vulnerable to an unwanted emotional response. An intense emotional response on my part runs the risk of shifting me away from the de-centred but influential position. Once I identify these potential therapeutic pitfalls, I can decide which measures to take to mitigate their unwanted influence over my work.

To provide an example, the following is a partial list of significant life events I have identified that have the potential to interfere with my work in the therapy session:

- A skiing accident where my teenage daughter sustained a life-threatening brain injury

- Expecting my first child while working at a child sexual abuse program
- The unexpected death of a much-beloved aunt
- Bearing witness to a family member's struggle with depression

All of these experiences have had a high emotional charge for me and therefore have the potential to put me at risk for experiencing an intense emotional response when working with an individual who has experienced a similar circumstance. Listing them is an important step that increases my awareness and allows me to take preventive measures as needed. Preventive measures can range from doing grounding breath work practices prior to a session, to inviting a co-worker to join me in the session, to referring the individual to another practitioner.

To clarify, I do not want to give the impression that any traumatic life event can be completely mitigated by these fairly basic self-care practices; some life experiences require more intensive and extensive support. But I find that an informal self-assessment of vulnerability helps to decrease the risk of my emotional response moving me away from the de-centred but influential position.

CLINICAL CONSULTATION

When doing trauma work, I make extra effort to access a clinical consultation team. That is, I have a few trusted colleagues who are skilled and knowledgeable about trauma and whom I can call upon when doing this kind of work. I choose individuals who know me well enough to have an idea about what my vulnerabilities might be and are willing to bring these to my attention.

Relying on colleagues' support to manage complex situations is likely a familiar practice for almost all practitioners. Again, I highlight it here as being particularly helpful for enhancing safety for individuals who are working with the effects of trauma.

One example that illustrates the value of having a clinical consultation team comes from my work in an educational therapeutic program serving adolescents and young adults. The program had a dozen highly qualified staff that included several teachers, a social worker, family support workers, and a clinician (me). In this work context, all of the staff formed the clinical consultation team. It was a dream team.

During one particular staff meeting, I learned that the program had just accepted a 19-year-old female. She had been seriously injured in a car crash two years prior and was struggling to recover from this life-changing, traumatic event. Immediately, a little bell went off in my brain and a corresponding nervous flutter started in my gut. I realized that this young woman was about the same age as my daughter and the timing of the automobile collision was similar to that of the ski crash during which my daughter had sustained a serious brain injury.

I noted my response to some of the parallels and also noted that I was able to maintain my composure. However, as the case worker provided more details about the young woman's situation, I realized that a bizarre coincidence was unfolding. I was transported back to the terrible night in the hospital's emergency receiving area where my husband and I had stood at my daughter's side as she lay inert, unconscious, and battered on the stretcher.

We kept vigil there for hours, waiting for a bed to become available in the intensive care unit. As a consequence, we witnessed several emergency scenarios unfold before us as ambulance after ambulance brought seriously hurt individuals into the area for immediate medical intervention. In those kinds of close quarters, you cannot help but see and hear what is going on.

As I heard more about the young woman joining the program, I realized that she was one of the critically injured individuals I had seen that night. I hadn't known her name, but I vividly remembered her situation; it had just been so similar to my daughter's. Once I figured this out, that wee bell in my brain became a gong and the flutter morphed into a lump of dread. I no longer felt composed.

Fortunately, I was supported by my stellar consultation team, and we were able to debrief this clinical issue and create a plan of care that would ensure safety for the student. As it turned out, I did not end up working directly with the young woman. However, anticipating my potential involvement and creating a team plan around it helped me to feel assured that her safety was protected.

From a personal perspective, I was able to take this experience and use it to further my own personal healing around my daughter's injury. From a professional perspective, it also acted as a warning for me: I must be mindful of the charge that is still attached to this personal incident and continue to work to mitigate any negative influence it could have on my work with individuals in future sessions.

Practices Used at the Time of the Session

The work I did with Josie, a 19-year-old female, illustrates how I used self-care practices during our sessions. These included the review of session notes, body scans, and constructive breath work.

Josie, who had sustained a serious concussion while playing soccer, came to see me about her post-injury struggles. The consequences of the concussion were dire for Josie. Prior to the injury, she was a fully engaged, high-achieving high school student with a close circle of friends. She was also an elite-level, competitive soccer player.

Josie's recovery from the head injury was slow and painful. For over a year, she was not able to attend school or participate in physical activity of any kind. Her career in competitive soccer—the passion of her young life—was indefinitely delayed and quite possibly finished.

After the year of recuperation, Josie returned to her high school. She found that she was unable to concentrate on her academics, she missed soccer terribly, and she missed her friends who had moved on to the next grade. She became overwhelmed with feelings of hopelessness and despair. Being back at her old high school just did not work for her. It was at this point that she began to work with me.

REVIEW OF INFORMATION AND SESSION NOTES

Before meeting with Josie, I reviewed the referral information with an eye for ferreting out potential areas of my own vulnerability. I searched for any content that presented an emotional charge for me. I looked for any themes in Josie's life that may also be present in my own life. In other words, I checked for areas that

I had previously identified as potential pitfalls for me in my informal assessment of vulnerability. Was there any material in Josie's documentation that had the potential to interfere with my ability to be fully present and of service to her?

In Josie's case, I made note of several facts about her situation that were similar to those of my daughter's: Josie's gender, the seriousness of her head injury, the age at which Josie sustained the injury, her difficult and lengthy recovery, the potential loss of her life's passion (my daughter's being dance), and her pre-injury high academic achievement and positive social adjustment.

BODY SCANS

After reviewing the notes, I scanned my body, focusing my attention from head to toe, tuning into any sensations (e.g., bodily tension) that might indicate an emotional response to the information I had just read. I focused my attention more on those areas of my body that I know regularly alert me to the presence of emotion: back of the neck, upper chest, and abdomen. Then, I reviewed the information again and scanned my body a second time to ensure that any emotional charge was either nullified or insignificant. In Josie's case, I found no indication of tension or emotional charge.

I have found that if I do notice an emotional charge in response to an individual's case history material and it is fairly minimal, these steps—review, body scan, repeat—are usually all that is required to achieve the objective of feeling solid and grounded. Often awareness of the connection is enough to reduce the influence of the emotional charge.

However, if I continue to experience any kind of unwanted emotional response, then I proceed with a brief mindfulness exercise with the intention of rendering the emotionally charged material inert, at least for the duration of the upcoming session.

After a couple of sessions of working with Josie and implementing this pre-session protocol, I felt that the emotional charge associated with any information connected to her had been thoroughly dealt with. Moving forwards with the work, I did not feel it was necessary to keep previewing the session notes.

I continued to use the body scan before subsequent sessions with Josie because of its utility in alerting me to any kind of new sources of tension that have the potential to disrupt the work. For example, I may have identified body tension that originated from recent life experiences like the low-grade worry that my teenage son was home from school with a fever, the frustration over a petty argument with my spouse as I left the house, or even something as mundane as the irritation at being delayed in traffic on the way to the office. In this way, the body scan was and continues to be a general tool that helps me notice the tension of everyday life, address it, and show up in a session with a calmer, clearer, and more grounded presence.

I also sometimes use body scans during the session as a quick check-in measure for myself. At first, this can be tricky to learn to do as it requires one to shift one's attention away from the individual to oneself. However, I have found it has become easier over time.

The body scan I use during a session is fast and fairly superficial, lingering only on key zones (back of the neck, chest area, and abdomen) where I typically hold tension. In this way, I use the body scan as a self-monitoring device, which helps me to maintain a grounded presence. I also coordinate my personal body scans to occur at the same time as the check-ins that I regularly do with the individual.

Finally, I often do post-session body scans. After the individual has left, I take a few moments to sit quietly and do a quick body scan. This helps me to identify any indicators of discomfort, dissatisfaction, or uncertainty I may have about the session. Scanning helps me check for two main problem indicators: my energy level and my sense of completion.

If my energy level is overly depleted and I feel drained, my experience tells me that I was likely taking on too much responsibility for the individual's work. Conversely, if I feel inspired and energized at the conclusion of a session, it means I have most likely found that sweet spot of supporting the individual to do their own work.

Noticing my energy level is a gauge for measuring my groundedness during the session. As well, if a body scan uncovers a feeling of unfinished business or a sense of unease about the session, this can be a sign that I need to take an extra step with regard to the individual's safety.

Identifying this sense of dissatisfaction with a session then leads me to consider options for addressing it. For example, in Josie's case, I could have consulted with my clinical consultation team about the work we did. I might have followed up with Josie between sessions to see how she was doing, or with her permission I may have invited one of the team members to join the next session.

Alternatively, it may be enough just to make a note of this feeling of dissatisfaction and do extra preparation prior to the next session. That is, I could have done some constructive breath work (see examples below) and focused intention-setting prior to working with Josie again.

In general, I use body scans as a self-monitoring tool. They help me notice any kind of tension or discomfort that might interfere with the work and allow me to address it in the moment. Addressing the tension or discomfort can range from setting an intention to push it aside to adjusting my breathing rate to taking some time out for a mindful exercise such as constructive breath work, the 5-Minute Breathing Task, or a short meditation.

CONSTRUCTIVE BREATH WORK

If after previewing the individual's information with the accompanying body scans, I find any lingering emotional charges, I then turn to constructive breath work. Similar to the therapy application, I use constructive breath work to:

- Transform any troublesome thoughts and
- Punctuate the commitments I have for the upcoming therapy session.

Below is what constructive breath work could look like for the Josie example. I would say the following statements out loud followed by a deep, slow inhalation and exhalation.

> *I recognize and acknowledge that Josie's situation has several parallels to that of my daughter. <breath>*
>
> *I can work in a way that is of service to Josie even though her brain injury and challenges around recovery remind me of*

my daughter's brain injury and her challenges with recovery. <breath>

I know that any lingering upset, fear, or worry that I still carry from my daughter's brain injury experience is not intense or powerful enough to interfere with my work with Josie and the challenges associated with Josie's brain injury. <breath>

I know that I have done the personal work with regards to my daughter's serious ski crash and brain injury such that it no longer has the same intense emotional charge that it used to have for me. <breath>

However, I recognize there is some residual emotion regarding my daughter's injury that I am still holding on to: an extra protectiveness. This is something that I am not interested in changing right now. I do know that I am no longer holding on to the intense feelings of fear and anguish that I experienced following the incident. <breath>

I know that this protectiveness feeling will not get in the way of my work with Josie. <breath>

I set the intention that my experience with my daughter will only enhance my capacity to be an empathic counsellor with Josie. <breath>

I set the intention that I can be solid and grounded when working with Josie. <breath>

> *I also set the intention that I can set aside or "park" any residual stress or upset that still lingers for me such that it does not enter into my work with Josie today. <breath>*

Setting aside or parking any personal "static" is a useful intention-setting tool. I have found it works best if I include the commitment to address whatever it is at a later time and then follow through with that commitment.

I also use constructive breath work in a general way to set the intentions for an upcoming session even if there are no concerns for me to address. In the case of Josie, I might use the following intention-setting constructive breath work statements:

> *I am grounded and calm and in a place to be of service to Josie as she does her work today. <breath>*
>
> *I am ready to work in a grounded and calm manner so as to be better able to work effectively with whatever Josie brings to our meeting. <breath>*

For practitioners who have a more spiritual inclination, creating a brief centring prayer with breath work serves the same purpose. There was a time in my spiritual life where I found this prayer version of the strategy resonated with me more:

> *Dear God, help me to be the best therapist I can be for this person who is coming to work with me today. <breath>*
>
> *Let my faith be an anchor for my work today. <breath>*

Dear God, guide me to be of service in a way that allows me to support the individual to do their own work in a safe and caring manner. <breath>

Dear God, please help me to stay de-centred as I work with this individual today. <breath>

And if despite all my efforts, things should go off the rails, God, please help me to use my faith to get back on track in a safe, caring, and respectful manner. <breath>

Amen. <breath>

Concluding Thoughts

Practitioner self-care and safety practices are additional ways that one can buttress the therapeutic relationship. All roads lead back to the therapeutic alliance. I recognize that practitioners likely already have some kind of self-care and safety regimen in place. My intention is merely to underscore the need for greater vigilance and care in developing these practices when one is working with trauma.

I believe that safety needs to be shored up from both sides of the therapeutic relationship. As practitioners, we are in a sense creating a safe place of shelter for individuals to do their healing work. Consequently, practitioner safety measures—self-monitoring, self-regulation, and general self-care skills—are another way to create a solid foundation for this type of work.

CHAPTER 4

Framing Up the Structure: Externalizing and Re-authoring Conversations

"**BLACK TAR. THAT'S WHAT IT FEELS LIKE.** It's thick and heavy. It sits in my chest. It has this tremendous pull. It is suffocating. It is smelly. It is hard to get away from."

Julia's voice had dropped to a lower, slower cadence, thick with emotion. She was gesturing to her chest and neck area as she spoke. Her body had stilled and tensed, becoming alert and guarded as the memory of the Black Tar was evoked. Her words spawned in my imagination a most fearsome image of a relentless, dark, and deadly entity. I pictured a version of J. K. Rowling's nefarious dementor.

I was very curious about this entity and, in particular, about how Julia had managed to live her life with a force such as this around. She had, in her clear and forthright way, created a powerful expression of the effects of childhood sexual abuse. Narratively speaking, she had externalized the problem.

Externalizing and re-authoring conversations that deal with the effects of a traumatic experience are central to building a solid framework upon which the "heavier" and more complex work of the core trauma work will rest. The process of externalization involves responding to the individual's concerns in ways that assist in separating the person's problems from their personal identity.

This kind of practice does not seek to eliminate, vanquish, or beat the problem. On the contrary, it assumes that problems are a natural part of a person's lived experience. Externalization of the problem allows individuals to view it in such a way that they are able to thoroughly describe it and map its influence.

The problem's influence can be mapped from many angles and on many levels. Mapping involves detailing the problem's effects on the individual's perceptions, thoughts, feelings, and behaviours, and it also involves exploring its effects on broader aspects of the person's life, such as relationships, work aspirations, and personal well-being.

Additionally, the effects themselves can then be viewed as problems to be externalized. For example, if the hardship experience is identified as "the problem" and anxiety and distrust in relationships are identified as effects of the problem, then these effects can also be viewed as problems to be externalized and their influence mapped. The result is the unfolding of several layers of exploration and mapping.

In this way, the individual creates an account of the problem that is particular, comprehensive, and personally relevant. The understandings gained from this account allow the individual to take a clear position in relation to the problem. That is, the person is able to commit to the idea of taking a stand in relation to the problem as well as elucidate why and how to accomplish this. This process is a means of deconstructing (or unpacking) the problem while simultaneously fostering a greater sense of personal agency.

During the course of the externalizing conversations, individuals can identify the times when they exerted influence over the problem. These identified exceptions, linked over time and circumstance, form the basis of a re-authoring process whereby an alternative story of resistance and competency is created. This re-authored story is more in keeping with the individual's preferred values, commitments, hopes, and dreams, and provides an alternative to the problem-saturated account that had previously dominated the person's lived experience.

This is only a brief description of these narrative practices for the purpose of creating context for describing the therapeutic journeys. For a comprehensive discussion of externalizing and re-authoring practices, I refer you to the work of Michael White[30] and Alice Morgan.[31]

In this chapter, I illustrate externalizing and re-authoring conversations by describing the therapeutic process of three individuals: Julia, Grace, and Cory. I begin by sketching each of their stories onto Michael White's "statement of position map,"[32] which includes the four categories of inquiry for externalizing conversations:

1. Negotiating a particular experience-near definition of the problem
2. Mapping the effects of the problem
3. Evaluating the effects of the problem's activities/influence
4. Justifying the evaluation

I then move on to a description of the re-authoring process that emerges from the externalizing work. I conclude with a

30 White, M. (2007). *Maps of narrative practice*. W. W. Norton & Company.

31 Morgan, A. (2000). *What is narrative therapy? An easy-to-read introduction*. Dulwich Centre Publications.

32 White, M. (2007). *Maps of narrative practice*. W. W. Norton & Company. pp. 38–59.

description of how each individual incorporated breath work safety practices to facilitate their work.

Julia's Work

EXTERNALIZING CONVERSATIONS

Julia had participated in several courses of therapy over the span of her adult life. From the outset, she was very clear about her intentions for our work together as evidenced by her response to my usual first-session query of "What are your hopes for our work together?" She stated that she was looking for a "reset" for her life. She described herself as "hitting a wall" in terms of "being tired of being tired," of feeling a certain "emptiness in life," and of "generally feeling low."

She also stated that she was feeling disconnected from those around her and that she was experiencing a great deal of anxiety. Further, she said that she was tired of feeling hopeless and not experiencing the relief she was looking for, despite her efforts to make herself feel better.

As well, Julia described her current situation as being strongly linked to the sexual and physical abuse she experienced as a child. She declared that the status quo as she described it to me was not okay with her, and her primary reason for meeting with me was in an effort to change it. Her comprehensive and well-articulated response suggested to me that she had invested considerable time, energy, and thought into what she wanted from therapy. As time would tell, Julia's tenacity, thoughtfulness, and willingness to engage in the therapeutic process would continue throughout our work together.

After Julia outlined her hopes, we then moved on to addressing therapy worries. I described this part of Julia's work earlier (see Chapter 2). Navigating the therapy worries work provided Julia with an added sense of purpose and confidence.

Negotiating a Particular Experience-Near Definition of the Problem

Julia struck me as a woman of lively intellect and dogged determination as she fully embraced the work with me that led up to her articulation of the Black Tar. As mentioned, she had addressed several therapy worries and had begun to incorporate the breath work into our conversations. Now, she was eager to turn her attention to those concerns that had brought her to therapy in the first place.

We began the externalizing conversation that was aimed at gaining a more thorough understanding of the problem and its effects on her life, which eventually led to naming the problem: the Black Tar. I started by reiterating some of the effects of childhood abuse that Julia had already presented to me:

> *Julia, you mentioned earlier that some of the impacts* [effects] *of the childhood abuse you are currently experiencing include a Tired-of-Being-Tired Feeling, Emptiness, and a State of Feeling Low, Disconnection, and Anxiety. As well, you mentioned that you are interested in gaining some relief from these effects and that you have already expended considerable effort towards that end: previous therapy, reading relevant literature,*

> *and attending self-help workshops. In an effort to head in the direction of gaining some relief from these impacts, could you first explain to me a bit more about how they are showing up in your life right now?*

In this, I had editorialized the information that Julia provided. But I stuck as close to her words as possible while changing the structure of the words so that the feeling states were more amenable to externalization.

It was at this point that Julia responded with the vivid description of the Black Tar of past abuse. It is worth repeating: "[It's like] Black Tar. That's what it feels like. It's thick and heavy. It sits in my chest. It has this tremendous pull. It is suffocating. It is smelly. It is hard to get away from."

With this response, Julia had articulated a particular experience-near definition of the problem. Naming the problem directly or through metaphors (e.g., the Black Tar) and then further developing a useful externalization of the problem is one of the early tasks of the narrative therapist during externalizing conversations.

Julia's vivid metaphor made it easy for me to join her in uncovering the specific attributes and qualities of the Black Tar. She provided much of the information spontaneously, but some of the questions I asked her included:

> *How long has the Black Tar been around? How often does it show up?*
>
> *Are there certain times when it is more intense? Less intense?*

Could you tell me more about what it is like for you when the Black Tar makes an appearance?

Do you get any warning that the Black Tar is going to show up? Is it a sudden visitation or does it creep up on you gradually? Or does it vary?

Can others tell when the Black Tar is around? Does anyone else know about it?

It is important to note that, in practice, I do not present questions like these (or any questions, for that matter) in rapid-fire succession. Rather, the individual's response to each question is an opportunity for exploring the particulars of their experience and for furthering rich story development. That is, these questions lead to opportunities for loitering with intent, for thickening the preferred story.

I have learned that an externalization can show up in a myriad of ways. It often emerges during an exploration of the nature of the problem while I am gathering an understanding of the particulars of the problem and how the problem shows up in the individual's life. Like an image that gradually comes into focus as the lens of a camera is adjusted, so also does the externalization become more defined and understood as the externalizing conversation unfolds.

Other times, externalizations seem to make a sudden, more dramatic entrance into the therapeutic conversation, forming quickly and substantively and boldly taking centre stage in the conversation. Julia's Black Tar externalization falls more into this second category.

Mapping the Effects

Learning about the specifics of the Black Tar very naturally led into a conversation where Julia was able to map the effects it had on her life. Following are some questions I asked to explore the Black Tar's effects:

> *How does the Black Tar influence your day-to-day life?*
>
> *How does the Black Tar impact how you feel emotionally?*
>
> *Can you tell me a bit more about how the Black Tar impacts how you feel physically?*
>
> *How does the Black Tar impact how you think or what you think about?*
>
> *How does it impact what you say and do?*
>
> *How does the Black Tar affect your relationships with your kids, your husband, your friends, and yourself?*

Julia's responses to these questions revealed that the Black Tar was pervasive. Recently, it had been showing up every day. As well, it had been around for many years. Though it had come and gone over the years, for the past three months it had been around much more. Often, it hung around for several hours in a row.

The Black Tar affected her emotionally and physically. It brought with it Anxiety, Hopelessness, Despair, and Overwhelm. At times, the Black Tar made it difficult for Julia to breathe, and it brought a weighted heaviness to her chest. As well, it sucked the energy out of her and made her feel exhausted. Some days, the Black Tar made it difficult for her to do even the most basic tasks around the house.

At this time, Julia described the Black Tar's influence as very debilitating in that it was making her not want to shop, cook, leave the house, or care for her children. It made her not want to see anybody. It brought with it several other compatriots—Irritability, Disconnection, and Excessive Worry. Julia noted that she was most concerned about the way the Black Tar could interfere with her ability to care for her children and to care for herself.

These discoveries led to more questions geared towards further mapping the effects of the Black Tar and the externalization of some of those effects:

> *Anxiety, Hopelessness, Despair, and Overwhelm—how do these show up for you? Do they team up together or do they show up separately? How do they affect your ability to take care of your children, your home, and yourself on a day-to-day basis? Can you rank them in terms of their level of influence on your life right now, say, on a scale of 1 to 10 where a 1 equals low influence and a 10 equals high influence?*
>
> *Irritability, Disconnection, and Excessive Worry—how do these show up? All together or individually? How are they similar to or different from Anxiety, Hopelessness, Despair, and Overwhelm? Do some show up more than others? If so, how? Which ones are more influential? Is there a ringleader or do they all work equally in concert together?*

Julia described in some detail the ways that these effects of the Black Tar were impacting her family life and her personal life. She ranked Exhaustion and Excessive Worry as two of the most influential of the effects. She concluded that focusing on ways to take charge of these effects would go a long way towards also reducing the unwanted influence of the Black Tar.

Evaluating the Effects and Justifying Her Evaluation

As mentioned earlier, Julia came to her first meeting with me having already completed a great deal of personal work regarding her concerns about the effects of child sexual abuse on her life. As a consequence, our initial conversation began with Julia's assertion that she was fed up with the effects of childhood sexual abuse and their interference with her ability to have the life she wanted.

That is, Julia started our work together with an evaluation about the effects and by expressing her conclusions about how they were problematic for her. She had also taken a firm position in that she articulated that she wanted something different from what these effects had to offer her. Once we had explored the influence of the Black Tar in some detail and gained a richer understanding of its effects on her life, Julia and I revisited her idea of wanting something different in her life.

RE-AUTHORING CONVERSATIONS

The idea of wanting something different in her life led to us exploring together the following kinds of re-authoring questions:

> *The fact that you want this situation with the Black Tar to change and, in particular, that you want to change the way that the Black Tar interferes with your ability to take care of your children, what does that say you want for yourself? What does that say that you value in relation to mothering and your children?*
>
> *And the fact that you are not okay with the Black Tar's ability to get in the way of your own desires and self-care, what does that say you want for yourself instead? What does that say about what you want for your life?*
>
> *And you mentioned a feeling of Disconnection that is also a result of the Black Tar's influence—an effect that you described as frustrating for you. So, what does this say you want for yourself in terms of feeling connection in your life?*

From these questions, Julia articulated some ideas about what she valued in life and what she wanted to create more of for herself: being a supportive wife and a present, nurturing, and caring mother. Julia also identified that she desired to make room for the creation of a fulfilling life beyond these roles of wife and mother. She identified that she wanted a greater sense of connection with others, a greater sense of personal peace and happiness, and to be more self-loving.

We then discussed how Julia had already taken steps in the direction of nourishing these cherished values and commitments. That is, she was able to identify times when the Black Tar did not interfere with some of her values and commitments (unique outcomes and exceptions to the problem story).

As she described these positive exceptions, she also began to reacquaint herself with some of the personal skills and knowledges that she had utilized in the distant and recent past. This part of the conversation involved exploring the following types of questions:

> *Can you think of a time in the recent or distant past when the Black Tar's influence was weaker or less pervasive? Even for a short time? What was happening for you then that might have helped to keep the Black Tar in abeyance or weakened its hold on you?*
>
> *Can you think of a time when you were able to take action in terms of being a present and caring mother to your children despite the influence of the Black Tar? Can you describe that to me?*
>
> *Can you describe a time, even if it was brief, when you felt more connected to people in your life? How did you manage that given the presence of the Black Tar? How were you able to make that possible?*
>
> *Can you think of any initiatives of self-care or self-love that you have been able to take despite the presence of the Black Tar? How did you manage that?*

Julia generated several examples of times when she was able to stand up for what she valued despite the presence of the Black Tar, both in the distant past and more recently. Recent initiatives, which she saw as signs of heading in the right direction in terms of what she wanted for herself, included:

- Bringing her son to therapy,
- Making a connection with me for therapy for herself,
- Inviting her dear friend to come visit her and help her sort out her house,
- Inviting her beloved sister to support her in a therapy session, and
- Nurturing her skill and passion as a pianist by taking private lessons and volunteering to play piano for the drama production at her son's school.

These are a few of the many initiatives Julia was able to identify, all of which she saw as supporting the commitments and values she had articulated earlier.

APPLICATION OF BREATH WORK

The use of breath work during externalizing and re-authoring types of conversations serves to punctuate and deepen newly constructed understandings. In Julia's case, she found this meaning-based use of breath work extremely helpful and chose to incorporate it regularly into all aspects of therapeutic conversations.

For example, once she had articulated an idea that was important to her—like those values that she holds to be precious and dear—she would ask to incorporate breath work with a statement (or series of statements) that captured the essence of her idea. As well, she made a habit of bringing her notebook to our meetings, and she often would take the time to jot down the breath work statements that she found especially meaningful.

The following are some examples of the breath work statements Julia created and then jotted down for herself:

> *In the past, I have found ways to solve difficult problems, and I can put that skill and knowledge into figuring out how to be in charge and manage Excessive Worry and Exhaustion right now and moving forwards. <breath>*
>
> *I am a woman who values being a present, caring mother, and I am open to learning ways of further developing and nurturing this in myself. <breath>*
>
> *I am a woman who values being connected with others in my community, and I am ready to learn ways to nurture my current connections with friends and neighbours. <breath>*
>
> *I have been a supportive wife for many years, and I am interested in learning new ways to balance that role with self-care and the exploration of my own personal passions and interests. <breath>*

Sometimes the uncovering of cherished values and new commitments to these values brought with it some worry around how Julia would sustain the initiatives. Similar to the therapy worries that Julia addressed at the beginning of her first session, this ongoing kind of worry is concerned about the process of change.

Consequently, she found it useful to recondition some of the statements she had used previously and revisit them with the breath work in relation to her current thoughts and ideas. That is, the statements were similar, but she customized them to reflect the particular pieces that she was working on at the time. For example:

> *I can honour my pace of change with respect to figuring out how to balance my mothering, spousal, and self-care roles. I don't have to figure it out perfectly right away. <breath>*
>
> *Just because Excessive Worry and Exhaustion have been around for a long time doesn't mean it has to take a long time before I can experience some relief from their influence. <breath>*
>
> *I understand that developing connections with people in my community takes time, and I give myself permission to take the time I need to build those connections. I can do this in small steps or big steps depending on my level of energy. <breath>*

I believe that incorporating breath work in an ongoing fashion as described above is a useful way of supporting individuals in sustaining the hard work of resolving trauma. The desire to incorporate breath work in this way has become a pattern that emerges with many of the individuals with whom I have worked.

I propose the idea that while teasing out the effects of trauma or hardship is central, addressing the worry component about managing these effects on an ongoing basis is also an important aspect of the therapeutic work. This application of breath work acts as a thickening agent for the individual's preferred story: firstly, by reiterating and clarifying the person's commitments and initiatives and, secondly, by reducing the influence of worry, fear, and doubt that sometimes attaches to and weakens these newly established commitments and initiatives. Loitering with intent by including breath work helps to further strengthen and sustain the preferred story.

SUMMARY OF JULIA'S WORK

1. Naming the problem and gathering a thorough and detailed understanding of it. For Julia, this was the childhood sexual abuse, which she vividly depicted in her description of the Black Tar.
2. Mapping the effects of the Black Tar, including its oppressive physical, emotional, and relational impacts. For example, its suffocating ways; the Anxiety, Exhaustion, and Worry that it brought into her life; and its interference with her ability to function in various roles.
3. Identifying those effects which were most problematic or influential such as Exhaustion and Excessive Worry.
4. Evaluating the effects, taking a position regarding those effects, and discovering why it was important for her to take this position. That is, Julia concluded that the Black Tar was a disturbing and disruptive presence in her life that was getting in the way of her ability to be the kind of mother, wife, and person she wanted to be.
5. Beginning the work of re-authoring as she further explored her position regarding the effects, thereby uncovering her desire to hold on to certain cherished values and desires:

to be a supportive wife and a present and nurturing mother, and to create a fulfilling life for herself outside of these family roles.

6 Continuing with re-authoring work by identifying and detailing steps she had already taken in spite of the problem's effects. For instance, despite the influence of the Black Tar, Julia came to therapy and connected with her sister.
7 Exploring new possibilities and initiatives in realizing her desires, for example, piano lessons and volunteer work at her son's school.
8 Applying the breath work practice to consolidate steps already taken and reinforce future aspirations and commitments.
9 Identifying the worry that accompanies this kind of effort and resolving this through breath work. For example, Julia used breath work statements to honour her own pace of change and remind herself of her proven ability to make changes.

Grace's Work

Grace struck me as a very gifted woman. She came across as motivated, clever, articulate, intuitive, and courageous. Grace is married to David, and they have three children: baby Georgie, 5-year-old Thomas, and 8-year-old Janelle. Grace works as an elementary school teacher. She had been referred to me by Tara, an associate of mine who is a massage therapist specializing in cranial sacral therapy.

During the course of her body work with Tara, Grace uncovered childhood hurts that still were having a significant impact on her. By coming to talk with me about these past hurts, Grace was looking for additional support for her healing process.

EXTERNALIZING CONVERSATIONS

Negotiating a Particular Experience-Near Definition of the Problem

In response to my opening query of "What are your hopes for our work together?", Grace had written "to heal from abuse and change family dynamics." I asked Grace to describe to me how abuse was related to family dynamics. She then disclosed that she was sexually and physically abused by her much-older cousin when she was a small child. Grace explained:

> *The past abuse I experienced from my cousin has made me anxious, frightened, and unwilling to be near him or connected to him and his family. He is married and has children, and I want our kids to play together. But I don't trust him, and I can't be around him, and I don't want my children around him either. I don't even want to be around him at larger family gatherings like weddings and Christmas anymore. Before, I could manage it—getting together with him and family. But since a recent incident when he had a huge anger outburst … it triggered the old memories of the past abuse. Now, I no longer want to have any contact with him.*

With the intention of checking that I had an accurate understanding of Grace's particular experience, I responded with the following editorial:

> *Okay, so can you tell me if I'm understanding things correctly? Does it make sense to say that the past abuse has made it very challenging to be around your cousin and his family such that you don't even want to be around them anymore? And that one of the consequences of the past abuse is distressing memories that are now getting in the way of you enjoying your extended family gatherings?*

Grace affirmed my take on her situation. After gaining this understanding of Grace's hopes for our work together, we then shifted gears to addressing therapy worries. Grace uncovered therapy worries similar to those articulated by Julia, and like Julia, she found the therapy worries work helpful. (For reference, see Julia's therapy worries work in Chapter 2.)

After moving through the safety practice of addressing therapy worries, Grace and I then returned to our conversation about her hopes for our work together. She further elaborated that she had recently been experiencing increased distress related to memories of the past abuse.

In turn, this had resulted in her feeling fearful of being around her cousin. She noted that she no longer looked forwards to extended family gatherings. Rather, she now wished to avoid these kinds of functions altogether because she didn't want to risk being in his presence.

This had deeply upset her on two accounts. Firstly, she was upset about missing out on family gatherings. Secondly, she was distressed by the constant fear and anxiety that had developed, which she was now experiencing in her everyday life.

From the onset of our conversation, Grace referred to the childhood abuse she experienced as "the past abuse." She continued to speak of "the past abuse" as the main problem from which her current concerns arose. Following her lead, I used this name for the problem, "the Past Abuse," as we engaged together in an externalizing conversation.

Mapping the Effects

We moved on to mapping the effects of the Past Abuse by exploring the following questions:

> *You described earlier that your cousin's recent actions triggered memories of his abuse of you as a child. Is it fair to say that some of the effects of the Past Abuse include distressing memories as well as Anxiety, Fear, and Distrust?*
>
> *Can you tell me a bit about how Anxiety and Fear related to the Past Abuse have shown up in your life? How have Anxiety and Fear shown up at home? At work?*
>
> *Have Anxiety and Fear shown up with respect to you and your husband? Have they shown up with your children? Your other family relationships? Your parents? How so?*
>
> *How have Anxiety and Fear affected the way you think?*

How have Anxiety and Fear affected your body? How have they affected your physical well-being? Do Anxiety and Fear show up in your body? If so, where and how? How often? What are the signs or signals that your body has been affected by Anxiety and Fear?

How often are Anxiety and Fear showing up? Every day? More in certain places or situations than in others?

Have Anxiety and Fear gotten in the way of what you want in life (e.g., relationships and physical, emotional, and mental well-being)? If so, what has been impacted/stifled/weakened in your life? What have Anxiety and Fear stopped you from doing, feeling, or thinking that you wanted to do, feel, or think?

Grace clearly identified Anxiety and Fear as the main effects of the Past Abuse, and I continued to explore these effects with her. I asked Grace several externalizing questions about Anxiety and Fear similar to those above. She articulated several ways that they were influencing her life:

- A stronger sense of fear when she is around her cousin but that persists when she is not in his presence
- The development of recurring fears of being triggered in the presence of her cousin
- Stomach distress
- Sleeplessness
- A general feeling of anxiety that is present most of the time; Grace described this as a feeling of being "out of control"

- An increase in worry thoughts about bumping into him in public places like the grocery store, the park, etc.
- An increase in worry thoughts about how her desire to stay away from her cousin and his family is potentially negatively affecting her children
- An increase in worry about her husband's worry for her
- The development of feelings of anger and resentment towards her parents related to not protecting her from the Past Abuse, and also concern about not knowing how to resolve this with them
- The development of worry and anxiety with regard to approaching her parents to talk about the issue; a fear of not being supported by them again now
- An increase in vigilance and worry about the children she teaches in her classroom
- Excessive feelings of agitation for her when children in her classroom "lose it" (i.e., get upset)
- An uncomfortable increase in emotional intensity when dealing with difficult issues with the children in her classroom, especially if she has concerns about child abuse or neglect
- Frequent fretting and anxious thoughts connected to abuse memories (e.g., "What's going to set him off next?")
- Boundary concerns between family members, especially between herself and her cousin and between herself and her cousin's wife
- Disappointment and sadness about the necessity of keeping her children separate from her cousin and his family

Evaluating the Effects and Justifying Her Evaluation

Grace started our work by presenting her evaluation of the problem, her position with respect to the problem, and why she was taking this position. That is, Grace had succinctly described the problem of the Past Abuse, said that she was unhappy with its impact on her life, and asserted that she wanted to change this state of affairs because it was interfering with both her family life and her own well-being. She wanted to "heal from abuse" and "change family dynamics."

My experience is that this clear kind of presentation of the problem does not often occur in the opening conversation, but it did for Grace. It speaks to the meticulous care and thought that she had already put into trying to understand her concerns.

After mapping some of the effects of the Past Abuse, we used the following questions to revisit Grace's initial hopes for her work with me:

> *I take it from our conversation that the degree to which the Past Abuse—along with its accompanying effects of Anxiety and Fear—is influencing various aspects of your life right now is not okay with you?*
>
> *Or in other words, this state of affairs—the influence that the Past Abuse is currently exerting on your life—is something you are interested in changing?*
>
> *So, is part of our work about you reducing the influence of Anxiety and Fear on your life and recovering more of a sense*

> *of "feeling grounded, calm, and the ability to be centred and at peace"* [These are Grace's words verbatim.] *in your life? Is that what you would like?*
>
> *And with regard to "healing from the abuse and changing family dynamics," does this include finding ways to manage or be more in charge of Anxiety and Fear, especially as it relates to your cousin and his family? Would that be of interest to you? Of value?*
>
> *And is working on how to manage and be in charge of Anxiety and Fear something you want to pursue in order to find more calm and peace in your relationship with your parents?*

RE-AUTHORING CONVERSATIONS

As a consequence of Grace's clarity, we very quickly transitioned into re-authoring kinds of exploration. The values and commitments that she held dear began to emerge. In particular, Grace spoke of how important family togetherness is to her and her husband within both the immediate and extended family spheres.

Grace identified the following life commitments and values that had been most disrupted by the Past Abuse and its effects of Anxiety and Fear:

- Her personal sense of feeling grounded and calm and her ability to be centred and at peace in day-to-day life
- Her confidence with parenting
- Her time and enjoyment with extended family
- Her comfortable relationship with her parents

- Her wish for a close-knit extended family
- Her confidence and ease in the classroom

Speaking with Grace about those aspects of her life that she cherishes and that also had been adversely impacted by the effects of the Past Abuse furthered the re-authoring conversation. The kinds of questions that led to the uncovering of these understandings were:

The fact that it is not okay for Anxiety and Fear to interfere with your life in the way they have, what does that say about you and about what you stand for in terms of family?

What does this say about what you want for your family? Your immediate family? Your extended family?

What does that say about you and what you value, this fact that you want to stand up to/change/manage Anxiety and Fear as they relate to family?

What does this say you want for your children? For your husband? For yourself?

How has this value of a close-knit family shown up in your life? When did it first appear? How does this value show itself now?

Can you think of some times in your life when you have been able to be in the family context without Anxiety and Fear interfering so much?

Can you think of any family interactions or situations when Anxiety and Fear didn't get to run the show, so to speak?

I learned more from Grace about how important family is to her:

- How she strives to create a safe and loving home for her children,
- How she wishes for her children to experience close and loving relationships with their grandparents,
- How she wants her children to have fun and playful connections with their cousins, and
- How she wants to be able to gather together for big extended-family gatherings where there is joy and fun, and love abounds and everyone feels safe.

Grace was also able to identify positive exceptions of family situations when Anxiety and Fear's influence was less disruptive to her. These included:

1. The times she spent nursing her baby during which she was able to experience peace and contentment,
2. When she successfully navigated the extended-family exchanges around her husband's birthday,
3. When she effectively managed family interactions around the visit of her younger brother, and
4. When she was able to have honest and clear communication with her cousin's wife.

APPLICATION OF BREATH WORK

As with Julia, Grace found the use of breath work very helpful. She utilized the breath work in several contexts: as a means of settling her body and mind; as a way to consolidate meaningful, newly acquired understandings uncovered in our conversations; and as a means of sustaining in her everyday life the work she did in the sessions.

In the first context, Grace made use of the 5-Minute Breathing Task (described in Chapter 2). This arose in a later session after I asked her my usual beginning-of-session questions: "What resonated for you from our work together in our previous meeting?" and "What would you like to work on today?"

Grace replied that the aspects of our last session that most resonated with her were the identification of those values and commitments that are precious and dear to her and the idea of the importance of safety in our work. She experienced the uncovering of those values and commitments as a profound learning for her. She saw them as central conceptualizations about who she is and who she wishes to be.

However, rather than continue with the re-authoring work around her values and commitments, Grace chose to first address issues of safety. That is, she wanted to address the fear and worry thoughts that were negatively impacting her day-to-day life. She described herself as feeling agitated and anxious most of the time during the day. As well, she was experiencing sleeplessness most nights. Her priority was to work on ways to better manage this agitation and anxiety.

When individuals report that anxiety, fear, or worry are impacting them in a pervasive way, I offer the 5-Minute Breathing

Task as a tool that could be helpful, and this is what I offered Grace. She was interested in learning about it, and so for the remainder of our session, we moved away from the re-authoring work and focused on learning the 5-Minute Breathing Task. This was one of those situations in which it made sense to me to pause the therapeutic conversation in favour of addressing safety concerns.

When Grace did the 5-Minute Breathing Task, she was able to slow her breathing rate from 22 breaths per minute down to 11 breaths per minute (one breath equaling one inhalation plus one exhalation). She noted that after completing this simple exercise, she felt calmer and more relaxed, both in her body and in her mind. Grace felt that she could take this tool home, play with it a bit, and see about using it during her day to help manage anxiety.

As with Julia, Grace also made use of breath work in a second context: to thicken or punctuate newly articulated commitments and understandings. In general practice, if I sense that an individual has expressed a particularly important understanding, I will check with the person to see if this is the case. If it is, I will then invite them to use the breath work in this consolidating manner.

When I first introduce breath work in this way, I provide a bit of an explanation. With Grace, it looked like this:

> *So, to summarize, family togetherness, both in the immediate family and the extended family, is a very important value for you, yes?*
>
> [Grace verbally agreed.]
>
> *I have found that pairing breath work with important understandings such as these helps to strengthen those understandings*

and settle them more securely into your body and into your mind. It can be a way of punctuating or integrating them or even strengthening them. Would you be interested in doing that right now?

[She verbally agreed.]

Grace paired the breath work with several of her own statements that she deemed particularly worthy of thickening. She crafted these phrases with me during our re-authoring conversations, and then she took them home in either digital or written format.

Following are some examples of her work:

I want to create more of the following in my life: feeling grounded, centred, calm, and at peace. <breath>

I know how to be grounded, centred, calm, and at peace. I do this when I am nursing Georgie, and I bring that knowledge forwards to help me learn how to manage Anxiety and Fear connected to the Past Abuse. <breath>

I am ready to learn new or more ways of managing Anxiety and Fear associated with the Past Abuse from my cousin. <breath>

I have been able to create healthy boundaries with my cousin, and I am open to learning ways to further develop this ability in relation to him and other family members, especially my mother. <breath>

I am a woman who cherishes the concept of family togetherness. <breath>

I can find new ways to further nurture the value of family togetherness. <breath>

Thirdly, Grace used breath work as a way to help her sustain her desired initiatives at home. She did this by creating prayers and applying the breath work while praying. This idea arose when we were exploring ways in which Grace had been able to calm herself in the past. Grace identified prayer as a powerful calming practice for her.

She set to work creating a bedtime prayer, one that incorporates breath work with statements that target whichever worry thoughts were currently holding unwanted influence over her. Following is a collection of the ideas and statements that Grace took home and transformed into bedtime prayers (See Appendix D for more examples.):

God, help me to release and transform the idea that I have to lose sleep about the worries to do with my cousin, family, the Past Abuse, children, etc. <breath>

Dear God, help me to learn that it's okay for me to take some time to learn these calming techniques. <breath>

Dear God, help me to embrace the knowledge that doing the breath work and learning to calm and soothe myself is part of my healing process. <breath>

Dear God, help me to accept that, even if I can't get to sleep right away, doing these relaxing breath work exercises is healing for my body. <breath>

I know that I need to figure out how to proceed with healing from the abuse by my cousin and that it will be confusing at times. I am committed to working through the confusion in ways that are healthier and better for me. And with God's help, I can tell my mind and body that this figuring out can happen tomorrow [or some other time] *with my husband* [or with a friend or whomever]*, and I don't have to dwell on it now at bedtime. <breath>*

I know that with God's help and with the help of my loved ones [She names friends and family.]*, I can find my way through to a calm place of healing. <breath>*

Dear God, help me to remember that I am a woman who can learn to let go of worry thoughts at bedtime. <breath>

I am a woman who can use my faith to help me learn how to let go of worry thoughts at bedtime. <breath>

Mind, I am grateful to you for being so vigilant, but now it is time to let go of vigilance and embrace quiet. You can be vigilant tomorrow during the day. For tonight, I hand this vigilance over to God's keeping. <breath>

> *My faith in God helps support me to learn new ways to be in charge of worry thoughts, busy thoughts, etc. so that they don't get in the way of good sleep. <breath>*
>
> *Dear God, help me to sustain my commitment to creating ways that will help me calm myself and get the healing sleep I want. <breath>*

As with Julia, Grace was very interested in using breath work in almost every aspect of her work with me. Whether it was doing the 5-Minute Breathing Task while nursing her baby or creating bedtime prayers, Grace creatively integrated breath work in ways that allowed her to gain more and more mastery over the effects of the Past Abuse.

SUMMARY OF GRACE'S WORK

- Externalizing the Past Abuse and mapping of its effects
- Addressing worries about the therapy process
- Further exploring the effects of the Past Abuse, particularly Anxiety and Fear
- Beginning the re-authoring work as she explored her opposition to the effects of the Past Abuse and what it meant in terms of her commitments to family. This included identifying positive exceptions of family scenarios where she was not overwhelmed by Anxiety and Fear.
- Learning restorative breath work techniques (e.g., the 5-Minute Breathing Task) to manage the ongoing anxiety and agitation she was experiencing during the day

- Continuing re-authoring work by using constructive breath work to punctuate and affirm newly articulated understandings and commitments regarding family
- Consolidating the re-authoring work by integrating prayer and breath work that were aimed at bolstering desired initiatives against the Past Abuse and in support of family connections

Cory's Work

Cory was a 17-year-old youth with a lean, wiry stature, delicate facial features, high cheekbones, and clear, expressive eyes. He displayed a serene and poised bearing that belied his current situation. His purpose in meeting with me was to find ways of dealing with the distressing effects of witnessing the murder of a man. The murder occurred in the context of a drug deal gone terribly wrong. Though Cory knew the murder victim, he did not know him well. Nonetheless, this experience proved to be a traumatic one for Cory.

Cory was familiar with facing challenges. He had been dealt a heavy hand of hardship in his young life—physical abuse and a disrupted home life were two themes running throughout his childhood. He was familiar with the child welfare system, and he had recently moved into a foster care–type of living arrangement.

Like many of the youth I have encountered with similarly complex and challenging backgrounds, Cory was an astute and laser-quick assessor of adults and new situations. But unlike many of the youth I have encountered in my work, Cory had a well-articulated set of spiritual and existential beliefs. This had something to do with his extensive yoga training. According to his mother, he was an old soul—wise, kind, and gentle spirited.

I learned that Cory was as intellectually adept as he was physically agile. Not only was he academically successful at school, he was capable of sophisticated and profound understandings. He was verbally gifted and struck me as a bit of a philosopher. He was also very artistic. Added to this mix was a dash of mischief and a well-developed sense of curiosity.

Cory liked challenges and to try new things. Perhaps this was what his mother meant when she noted that he liked to "test the limits." Regardless, Cory showed me several aspects of himself that filled me with a marvellous sense of hope and excitement about the work that we could accomplish together.

The single-session therapy I did in my early career has greatly informed almost all of my work. It has taught me ways to better focus and discern more efficient and respectful therapeutic paths to take based on an individual's wishes and readiness. When working with youth from troubled backgrounds in particular, this single-session experience has been invaluable.

During my career, I came to see one-on-one time with a youth as a precious gift of opportunity. I learned to maximize this time, knowing that it may be my only chance to meet with them. Or if I did get to see them again, it may be many months or years later. Such was the uncertainty of their life.

I sensed that my time with Cory was a similar kind of opportunity. I wanted to "make hay while the sun shines," as the expression goes. And looking at Cory from my therapist perspective, the sun was indeed shining. I was quite confident that we could accomplish a lot of work in a very short time. In the end, Cory turned out to be one of the fastest and most efficient individuals with whom I have worked.

One of the key reasons why Cory could cover so much ground involving such tricky and complex material was because he already had safety tools securely in place. His advanced training in yogic techniques meant that he was highly skilled in self-monitoring both his body and mind. This training also gave him extensive knowledge and practice with a range of breath work techniques. He already used breath work, not only for the purpose of creating inner peace and calm but also to explore and consolidate important values.

In other words, at the outset of our time together, Cory was already familiar with restorative and constructive breath work strategies. This allowed me to spend much less time with the safety aspects of the trauma work. Instead, I could move more quickly to the meaning-based work of externalization and re-authoring conversations and, in turn, to the core trauma work. For example, Cory did not need to address therapy worries.

EXTERNALIZING CONVERSATIONS

Negotiating a Particular Experience-Near Definition of the Problem

The first time I met with Cory, his entry into my office was more subdued than at subsequent meetings. He was accompanied by his foster parents who joined us for the first few minutes of our meeting.

I began with a version of the usual first-session question: "What are your hopes for our work together today?" The stunningly blank look Cory gave me in response led me to change gears quickly and suggest something a little less open-ended. I figured that my question was just too big and broad for him to manage at that moment. I chose to scaffold this question by asking a different one that was more structured and less all-encompassing:

> *It's okay not to know the answer to that question right now. In fact, I think it is a perfectly good use of our time right now to figure out the answer to that question together. Rather than starting with the answer, that can be our end goal for our work today. Does that sound okay to you?*
>
> [Cory nodded with a look of relief.]
>
> *So, you mentioned that you are here because you are really struggling as a result of witnessing the murder, right? Tell you what, it sometimes helps to get things going if I jot down a bunch of ideas that other people have brought in to work on. I can kind of brainstorm from my memory what others who have experienced very upsetting or terrible things have brought to work on, okay?*
>
> [He verbally agreed.]
>
> *And as I write these problems or concerns down, some may make sense for you, and you can let me know which ones those are. Some may not fit at all, and you can let me know that too. As well, doing this may prompt you to come up with different ideas that are more of a priority for you. If that happens, just let me know.*

With my single-session mindset firmly in place, I took a large piece of scrapbook paper, grabbed my pen, and set these on the table between us. I then jotted down some potential problems that people have identified in relation to hardship experiences. Cory chose the ones that fit for him and added a few of his own to complete his list: Stress, Worry, Anxiety, Sadness, Depression, Distraction, Fearfulness, Discontent, Anger.

After we completed this big list, Cory identified the problems that were exerting the most influence on his life. In order of most influential to least influential, he named Fearfulness, Anxiety, Discontent, Anger, Sadness, Depression, and Stress.

We then explored a few externalizing questions about each of the effects of the murder:

> *How does Fearfulness* [or Anxiety, Discontent, Anger, Sadness, Depression, or Stress] *show up in your life? At school? At home? With your friends? In how you think? In how you feel physically? In how you feel emotionally?*

As we explored some of these questions, Cory came to the conclusion that it is the presence of Anxiety in his life that best captures what he is experiencing. In other words, Anxiety is the main player, and the other feelings—Fearfulness, Discontent, Anger, Sadness, Depression, and Stress—play subordinate roles in his current life situation.

Mapping the Effects

He began to map the effects of Anxiety that had shown up since he had witnessed the murder. Following is a list of some of the most significant effects and how they impacted him:

- A strong physical component that showed up mostly in his gut in the form of stomachaches, discomfort, and nausea
- A physical and mental feeling of numbness or listlessness
- A feeling of helplessness, nausea, dizziness, and being "out of my body" associated with re-telling the story of the murder
- Difficulty with paying attention (his mind wandering a lot more)
- A preoccupation with a lot of "what if" thoughts (worry thoughts)
- The onset of disturbing dreams with themes of killing and death
- A propensity to get emotionally upset more easily
- The loss of a general sense of peace and contentment

Evaluating the Effects and Justifying His Evaluation

Cory moved through this part of the process with rapid-fire speed. He described losing a sense of peace and contentment in everyday life, qualities that he had worked very hard to cultivate through his yoga practice. That is, he had found that since he witnessed the murder, his usual skills and knowledges—the yogic practices of meditation and breath work—were no longer working for him.

He then indicated that this disruption was a huge loss for him, and the loss was not okay with him. He wanted to regain the sense of peace and contentment that was such an integral part of his life prior to witnessing the murder.

RE-AUTHORING CONVERSATIONS

Because Cory so quickly evaluated the effects of witnessing the murder and took a clear position regarding how he felt about these effects, he was able to then move into the re-authoring process. First, he identified that his ability to cultivate a sense of peace and contentment was something he highly valued in life. Next, he acknowledged that the qualities of calmness, happiness, and contentment were those that he most cherished, and they were commitments that he had spent a great deal of energy and focus on to develop in his life.

In a matter of two sessions, Cory zipped through the therapeutic processes of establishing a safe and workable relationship with me, understanding and implementing the breath work, joining me in an externalizing conversation that mapped the effects of witnessing the murder, and concluding with a re-authoring conversation that identified important commitments and values in his life: peace, contentment, happiness, and a sense of calm.

APPLICATION OF BREATH WORK

Cory did not use any of the restorative breath work techniques. He already had his own considerable repertoire of self-soothing breath work strategies firmly in place. He also had no need to do the pre-therapy worries work.

Rather, because he was so eager and confident, we were able to move directly into creating constructive breath work statements geared towards, first, putting the effects of witnessing the murder behind him and, second, revitalizing the commitments and values that are precious and dear to him that were adversely impacted by those effects.

Following are some of the constructive breath work statements that Cory created as part of our re-authoring conversation:

Peace and contentment are my deepest operating place. <breath>

Peace and contentment are like rocks at the bottom of a pond or a river, and the Anxiety thoughts are waves in the water, refracting and distorting the experience of the rocks. But I know that the rocks cannot be taken away from me. <breath>

And all I have to do is keep my attention on them, and I will be able see them with all their detail again. <breath>

I can trust in my faith that's based in my experience that the rocks of peace and contentment will always be with me and that their beauty is always accessible to me. <breath>

And if my focus on the rocks of peace and contentment is challenged in the future and the waves have returned to distort and refract my vision, I know that the nature of the rocks is constant, and I will be able to find the stillness and trust I need to bring peace and contentment back into view. <breath>

I am a person who knows how to cultivate peace and contentment, calm and happiness in my life. <breath>

Cory was unique in that he came to the therapy context with an advanced skillset for maintaining and sustaining his personal sense of equilibrium. That is, he arrived with his own elaborate set of safety tools already in place.

Comparatively speaking, he required much less from me to safely and confidently re-engage with those skills and knowledges. Very quickly, he was able to apply this expertise in our work together and move towards regaining the sense of peace and contentment that had been so shaken by the witnessing of the murder.

SUMMARY OF CORY'S WORK

- Externalizing and mapping the effects of witnessing the murder and generating an extensive list of effects that were both physical and emotional in nature
- Prioritizing some of the effects of witnessing the murder by ranking them in order of influence: Anxiety, Fearfulness, Discontent, Anger, Sadness, Depression, and Stress
- Exploring the effects of Anxiety in detail
- Creating constructive breath work statements geared towards putting the effects of witnessing the murder behind him
- Moving into re-authoring work by using constructive breath work statements aimed at revitalizing his commitments and values: his yoga practices and his desire to cultivate peace and contentment

Concluding Thoughts

Externalizing conversations are the stepping stones to re-authoring conversations. That is, once a person has deconstructed the problem by naming it, describing it, mapping its effects, taking a position of wanting something different from what it has to offer, and identifying why they want something different, the groundwork has been laid for discovering what the person wants instead—their preferred story. Re-authoring is a process of uncovering the cherished values and commitments of life that have been oppressed by the problem.

The re-authoring conversation centres around those times when the individual was able to stand up for these personal commitments in spite of the problem's influence. By gathering together and sequencing these positive exceptions and by focusing on the individual's ability to cope, the individual constructs or re-authors their preferred story of hope and competency. In privileging the person's abilities, skills, values, and commitments, this new story counters the negative identity conclusions fostered by the problem-saturated story and evokes the kind of personal agency essential in sustaining opposition to the effects of trauma.

The application of the breath work during externalizing and re-authoring conversations is as diverse and varied as the individuals with whom I meet. In the early stages when I sense a "therapeutic moment," I am likely to ask individuals if they think the breath work would be useful to add into our conversation. In this way, I learn when and how this safety tool fits for them. As individuals develop their own ways of using the breath work techniques, I shift to a more supportive position rather than a directive one.

I have noticed that including the breath work is helpful when the individual has experienced an "aha" moment—in other words, when a new understanding has suddenly become clear or acquired a more profound aspect. This can occur during any kind of therapeutic conversation, whether that be when one is connecting the dots about the impact of certain effects on one's relationships or articulating a heartfelt personal commitment for the first time.

I have found that individuals doing this kind of work often embrace the breath work components. They develop their own unique rhythm and style of integrating the breath work into our conversations, thus creating and customizing a practice of breath work that is uniquely their own.

The externalizing and re-authoring work in combination with breath work practices creates a structure strong enough to bear the weight of the heavy work that is yet to come. It is a kind of "framing up" of the individual's preferred story. It is built by gathering from individuals detailed information about the particular knowledges and experiences that they have acquired and utilized in their efforts to manage the effects of trauma.

This work is also about privileging those core values and most-cherished beliefs that underpin the person's skills and knowledges. Resting on a solid foundation of the therapeutic relationship, the structure of this work supports the individual to more safely move into the core trauma work.

CHAPTER 5

Scaffolding for Safety: Integrating Understandings to Support Core Trauma Work

"LISA, I CAN'T DO THIS!" Though spoken in a whisper, there was a knife edge of panic in my words that cut sharply through the short distance separating us. I directed this statement towards my friend and colleague. She and I share a passion for working with children and their families, and we endeavour to do this from a narrative practice perspective. It is what had brought us together that day.

We were sitting in a group of about 50 like-minded counsellors at a workshop[33] about receiving and responding to trauma and social suffering. The presenters were in the midst of introducing the material that they were going to share with us.

They instructed us to divide up into groups of three and to designate one person to be interviewed about a time when they were able to overcome hardship or challenge. Another person was to do the interviewing, and the third was responsible for transcribing the interviewee's words verbatim. We were all to take turns in each of the roles until we had three sets of transcribed stories about overcoming hardship.

Dread washed over me. It was not the idea of group participation that sent this wave of dread through my being. I am one of

---

33 Denborough, D., & White, C. (2009, April). *Responding to hardship: Collective narrative practice* [Workshop]. Dulwich Centre, workshop in Calgary, Alberta.

those interactive, social types who can embrace role play. Nope, it was the fact that I was two weeks out from one of the most challenging events of my life to date: the ski crash incident I have mentioned previously where my 17-year-old daughter sustained a life-threatening brain injury.

Now to be clear, the presenters specified that we were to choose a challenging example of hardship that was manageable and one that fit the workshop context. They assured us that they did not intend for us to bring fresh and potent personal struggles to the exercise.

The problem for me was that, though I desperately wanted to follow this dictum and generate a more benign example of overcoming challenge, I just could not get my mind or my body to cooperate. Each time I attempted to scan my memory banks for a minor challenge/hardship incident, I became agitated, and what filled my brain was the image of my daughter's battered and bruised form lying flat out on a stretcher. Help!

And that is exactly what Lisa did; she helped me to navigate this tricky situation. She and I formed a group of three with Maria, a counsellor from Mexico City whose life work was with women newly immigrated to Canada. Lisa's eyes locked briefly with mine, and she gave me a reassuring nod.

I turned to Maria and said, "I have had a difficult family situation recently, and because of that, I am just not up for doing the interviewee part of this task. If it's okay with you, I will pass on that part of the exercise, but I am happy to do the other parts."

"Of course, no problem," Maria responded with warmth and acceptance emanating from both her tone and posture.

We completed our modified version of the task and handed it into the presenter. The presenter collected these transcripts with the plan of transforming them into lyrics for a song that we would all sing during the last part of the workshop on the following day.

Fast-forward to the next day of the workshop. We had spent the first half of the day learning another methodology for receiving and responding to trauma and social suffering. After the lunch break, we turned our attention back to the songwriting exercise.

We assembled and sat down, forming a large circle. Our words, transformed into lyrics, were projected on a screen for all to see. With our voices, our various instruments from home, and our anticipation firmly in place, we launched into singing our collective song.

What transpired for me as I raised my voice, pounded my drum, and fully joined in is almost inexplicable. However, I will give my best attempt to describe what I experienced that day.

I felt transported. All the words I sang, though they were not ones that I had personally authored, I was able to embrace as my own. There was something universal in all of these particular accounts of overcoming hardship. So, though they were descriptions of individuals' personal and very specific experiences, they resonated for me nonetheless.

Some of the lyrics resonated more than others—like the drinking of tea with loved ones—as they more closely mirrored my own experience. However, even unfamiliar accounts of overcoming hardship also resonated with me on some level. I felt a palpable sense of connection to everyone in the room through the singing of their words. I also felt a sensation of being held in a collective embrace. It was a gentle but strong embrace and a respectful one—one that I felt I had given permission to receive.

I also felt buoyed up somehow by those around me. I hadn't even known I was drowning, but there I was being buoyed up in this wave of hope and caring. I felt this wonderful sensation of release and lightness that emanated from the centre of my chest. It occurred to me that I now fully understood what it meant to feel lighthearted. My heart had felt heavy, and this experience seemed to gently, cleanly, and compassionately lighten its load. I felt a deep sense of peace.

The song ended, and we all sat quietly for a few moments absorbing the experience. Then the workshop leader broke the silence by inviting us to share our impressions of what the singing of the song was like for us. I sat basking in my restful state. It occurred to me that since I had experienced something incredibly moving and profound, it was my responsibility to share this with the group.

However, I had made a promise to myself to stay in a safe and comfortable place during the workshop. Refraining from speaking of anything at all associated with my daughter's situation was working for me. I hesitated to speak now and risk disturbing the sense of peace and well-being that I had found. Several individuals shared about various positive effects of the singing of the song. I sat quietly, relaxing into the idea that I need not speak up.

I was just starting to congratulate myself for sustaining a listening and receiving mode for an entire workshop (very different from my usual modus operandi) when the woman sitting directly to my left spoke up.

"So, you have asked us today to choose a hardship to write about that was not too challenging, one that would be easy to manage in the workshop setting. So, it makes sense to me that I would get a lot of positive feelings and associations from this experience—just as others have also indicated. But what if someone has had a very recent, intense, and challenging experience?

One that is very painful and fresh? Would that person be able to get the same thing out of this as we have?"

I smiled inwardly. Clearly I was not meant to stay silent after all. Forces beyond my control were in play; some kind of ghost of collective Narrative Practice beckoned me to speak. So I spoke.

I tried to express all that I had felt during the song and afterwards. In his kind and gracious way, the workshop leader thanked me for speaking up and noted that, in doing so, I had highlighted one of the important aspects of this particular kind of collective practice: it allows those who cannot speak to be included in the process.

Shortly after the workshop, I embarked on my own healing process. At the time, I had every intention of seeking out a counsellor for this purpose. However, the physical aspects I was experiencing in the aftermath of the incident felt so immediate and intense that I decided to attend to these first.

My plan was to deal with the bodily tension and soothe the physical agitation that I had accrued since the incident. To do so, it made sense for me to turn to cranial sacral therapy (CST) for this. It is a modality that is comfortingly familiar to me, and I had found it effective in the past. I reasoned that once I had regained some physical composure, I would be in a better state to benefit from more conventional talking therapy.

To my surprise and relief, the re-authoring of my hardship experience naturally unfolded as I did the body work over the course of a few CST treatments. As the therapist identified sources of excessive bodily tension, I began to talk about the ski crash incident. With the support of the therapist's guiding questions and light touch, and with my framework of the absent but implicit firmly in place, a healing conversation ensued.

At the beginning of the first treatment, I had shared with the therapist my current state: post serious incident involving my child; feeling the effects of prolonged and acute worry, fear, and anguish; occasional flashbacks of my daughter in the emergency room; and my body feeling riddled with the stress and tension from all I had been through over the past days.

My hope for the session was to regain some of my physical composure that had been so disrupted by this incident, but I did not really know exactly what that might entail. I had a vague notion that I needed to do something to get rid of the flashbacks, the obsessive worry thoughts, my occasional bouts of feeling depersonalized and panicky—all those things that were so connected to my physical agitation.

At the time, I felt acutely aware (and wary) of the healing notion of "just letting go." I also understood that CST is about letting go of tension and releasing emotion. However, when I contemplated letting go of anything to do with my daughter's ski crash—whether that be tension, fear, worry, or negative thoughts and beliefs—my heart lurched in alarm. My body recoiled from this idea.

My logical brain said, "Letting go of this emotional stuff is a great idea! Let's do it!" My body's response said, "Asking me to let go of any of it right now is unconscionable; it is wrong to the bone marrow, wrong to the bottom of my heart, just plain wrong. You hold on to it! Grapple it to your heart! Bury it deep inside you where no one can take it!"

Fortunately, I also understood that one of the aspects of CST is that I get to decide when and what to release. During the conversation that accompanied the CST, I was able to resolve this inner conflict of letting go versus holding on. By utilizing the absent but implicit inquiry as a frame of reference, I articulated the cherished aspects of my life that were violated by this incident. These included the love for my child and my desire to be a good mother.

I was terrified at the thought of losing my daughter, and at some level, I felt responsible for not keeping her safe and being a "good" mother. I learned that my mother identity was crumbling in the face of the terrible truth that I have no way of guaranteeing my daughter's safety 100 percent of the time and that I never did have that ability.

Furthermore, the magnitude of the heart-wrenching distress I was feeling perfectly matched the magnitude of my love and devotion for my child. Loss or damage of something so important to me warranted this kind of pain and anguish. It made sense to hurt this much. The intensity of the pain felt like a form of honouring those cherished aspects of myself. And to want initially to hurt less or feel less somehow felt like a betrayal of my love for my daughter and, ultimately, a betrayal of my own most treasured values.

The horrible, debilitating anguish had gotten all tangled up with these beloved, beautiful aspects of my life. So, in the beginning, to let go of any distressing consequences felt just dead wrong for me. The risk that too much of the precious life bits would also be lost was not a risk I was prepared to take.

However, as I did the work of untangling what is precious and dear from the horror of its violation, I learned another piece: with the right kind of supports in place, letting go of parts of the physical agitation and emotional distress can feel completely right. And this type of process can lead to finding relief and even a sense of peace.

Unpacking My Personal Experience

Reflecting on my own experience, I was able to use my narrative practice framework to make sense of my own recovery process as I participated in the workshop and then again later as I did the body work during the CST treatments.

I viewed the collective song in the workshop as the place where I was able to begin the re-authoring process that would help create enough safety for me to approach the more challenging work later. That is, all the examples of how people overcame their past hardship—by drinking tea with friends, with their humour, by listening to their favourite music, and so on—were representations of life commitments and values that people hold dear, myself included. They were commitments of life to which I still held firm despite the hardship event.

When I began the CST treatments, I had my absent but implicit lens in place and was fortified by the re-authoring work provided by the workshop song. I believe this supported me to safely approach the question "What was it, that I hold as precious, was violated by the distressing experience of witnessing my daughter's life-threatening crash?" As I found my own answers to this central absent-but-implicit therapeutic question, I was able to transform the pain and anguish of the hardship incident and find some resolution and peace.

In terms of a physiological or bodily sense of safety, both the workshop and the CST practices soothed or calmed my body. In the workshop, singing the collective song and beating on the drum served this purpose. I experienced them as having a calming influence on my physical well-being. I received a similar calming benefit from the therapeutic touch of the cranial sacral therapist.

The workshop experience also underscored for me the importance of being in charge of my own processing of the hardship experience. That is, I got to decide how much and when I participated in the process, and this was key to feeling safe. At the time, the mere idea of doing the workshop task—discussing a past occasion of successfully overcoming a minor hardship—had thrown me into a tailspin. Essentially, it triggered a flashback or a kind of re-experiencing of the event.

This type of re-experiencing was threatening because I did not want or consciously choose to approach it. It did not matter that I had been directed to share only about a manageable experience. Just the idea of disclosing anything about hardship was still too close an association to my recent experience. I felt too raw and vulnerable to speak about any kind of hardship experience. My emotional response was extremely physical. It felt like too much too soon.

Then, the subsequent realization that I was not expected to jump into any kind of conversation associated with hardship was a great relief and restored to me a sense of safety. Again, the feeling of relief was very physical.

Like the workshop situation, the CST experience also underscored the importance of being able to choose what kind of work I wanted to do. This showed up for me when I encountered the experience of simultaneously wanting to hold on to and release tension associated with the hardship experience.

At the onset of the CST, letting go of anything to do with my daughter's crash was simply not a safe proposition for me. And I had felt comforted knowing that there was no expectation for me to do so. Later, as the therapeutic conversation unfolded and after I did the untangling work of separating the anguish from what is precious and dear, I was able to experience a considerable release of tension and agitation.

In both contexts, I learned firsthand that direct re-tellings of the hardship experience are not required in order to gain some measure of relief from its effects. I did not venture into a direct re-telling of the ski crash, yet at the conclusion of the workshop song I experienced an immediate sense of relief. After a few CST treatments, much of the agitation connected with the event, including flashbacks and elevated anxiety, had dissipated.

The sense of relief I had gained in both contexts had ushered in a sense of hope—the hope of finding a pathway through the swamp of fear and angst that the frightening event had dropped me into. All of this occurred without having to re-tell the particulars of the ski crash story.

I also learned that there is a safe time and place to do a re-telling. Shortly after I did this personal work, I found myself willing and able to recount in detail the story of the ski crash incident. I did this spontaneously and confidently at a celebration honouring the first responders on the ski hill whose timely and competent intervention played a critical role in my daughter's recovery.

And since that first successful re-telling, I have welcomed several opportunities to re-tell the story (to loiter with intent, as it were). It has become a kind of miracle story for me. It is a story of family, friends, and community coming together for a greater good. It has also become one of my most preferred of alternative stories.

A Re-conceptualization of the Trauma Experience

My personal experience of a hardship event and the subsequent healing journey gave me another vantage point for understanding the body-mind relationship as it pertains to trauma. The synchronicity of attending the workshop and then the CST treatments so near the time of my hardship incident yielded several practice shifts for me that were pertinent to how I work with trauma in general and absent but implicit inquiry in particular. That is, I was able to add understandings gained from my lived experience of a hardship event to my intellectual understandings about the trauma experience, which then informed how I thought about the absent but implicit inquiry and its application to trauma work.

And though I did not view my hardship experience as being as horrific or as enduring in comparison to those described by most of the individuals with whom I have worked, I did see some parallels with respect to how those individuals and I responded to the trauma experience. I concluded that the understandings that I gained from my personal experience might also be useful for others.

The central shift for me was the understanding of just how important a role a sense of safety plays—in particular, a physical sense of safety with respect to moving forwards with recovery. In terms of this bodily sense of safety, both the workshop and the CST included practices that soothed and calmed my body. In response, one of my main practice changes was to incorporate a parallel safety mechanism in Narrative Practice, namely body-mind practices such as the breath work discussed previously.

The workshop experience and CST experiences also underscored for me the importance of being in charge of my own processing of the hardship experience and how that is connected to a developmental progression of therapeutic tasks. That is, this feeling of personal agency occurred when I was able to participate in therapeutic tasks that were manageable for me and decline the ones that were just too much for me to handle. Then, once I had worked through certain aspects of my trauma response, I was able to move on and safely navigate more challenging aspects. There was a safe order to the progression of the work.

In short, my process of recovery emphasized for me the centrality of the individual's physiological response to a trauma experience and its connection to a sense of safety. It is much bigger than I had previously understood. This re-conceptualization of the trauma experience led to shifts in the way I work, many of which I have described in previous chapters. Later in this chapter, however, I tie together these understandings gathered from both my professional learnings and my lived experience and connect them to the idea of the absent but implicit. The end result is a set of practices specific to the core trauma work where safety is the top priority.

Integrating My Understandings into the Absent but Implicit Inquiry

Before illustrating the core trauma work practices with examples (upcoming in Chapter 6), I think it is useful to make explicit some of the conclusions I have arrived at regarding the concept of the absent but implicit, such as:

- The distinction between the type of absent but implicit inquiry that occurs during the earlier re-authoring conversations versus that which occurs during the later re-authoring conversations of the core trauma work,
- The importance of a bodily (physiological) sense of safety during the absent but implicit inquiry of the core trauma work, and
- The utility of following a developmental progression that involves scaffolding therapeutic tasks during the core trauma work so they are manageable from a safety perspective.

THE ABSENT BUT IMPLICIT INQUIRY: AN OVERVIEW

The understandings I have about the absent but implicit are based on the ideas articulated by Michael White[34] and further elaborated upon by Maggie Carey[35] and others. The absent but implicit refers to those intentions and preferred accounts of self that have been rendered invisible or have been subjugated by the problem story. These often neglected but preferred storylines are, in effect, "absent" (not explicitly expressed) in the individual's life, but they are "implicit" in that the expression of distress in relation to the

34 White, M. (2005, September 21). *Michael White workshop notes*. Dulwich Centre Publications. pp. 19–22. https://dulwichcentre.com.au/wp-content/uploads/2014/01/michael-white-workshop-notes.pdf

35 Carey, M., Walther, S., & Russel, S. (2009). The absent but implicit: A map to support therapeutic enquiry. *Family Process, 48*(3), pp. 319–331.

problem's influence implies that the individual prefers something different from what the problem story has to offer.

Narrative practices seek to uncover these absent but implicit storylines by engaging in the types of inquiry that explore the possibilities beyond the problem story. For example, in the case of an individual struggling with the problem of anxiety, questions that seek to explore those absent but implicit accounts of life could include:

- What does this say about you that you are not okay with Anxiety getting between you and your partner?
- What does that say you value in regard to your relationship with your partner?
- What does the fact that you are not okay with Anxiety's influence say about what you want for your life with your partner?

If anxiety is a problem and certain effects of it are not okay, this means there is something other than anxiety that the individual prefers. The uncovering of these other absent but implicit commitments and values leads to the development of alternative and, most importantly, preferred storylines of the self.

Though the absent but implicit is pertinent to all types of re-authoring conversations, I have found it to be a crucial organizing principle for the re-authoring conversations that focus on the individual's response to trauma. The concept of the absent but implicit offers the idea that a person's response to trauma, such as intense psychological pain or suffering, is an indication that something very important to them was violated or subjugated by the trauma experience.

The work becomes about uncovering and making explicit these absent but implicit cherished aspects of oneself that were subjugated by the trauma experience. Therapeutic conversations that use the absent but implicit in this way lead to the uncovering of the individual's preferred commitments, values, beliefs, and identities, and then to the re-authoring of their preferred story in relation to the trauma experience. I refer to this type of re-authoring conversation as the core trauma work.

One way of uncovering these cherished aspects of the self is by exploring the idea that the pain and anguish a person experiences in response to a trauma or hardship—be it mental, physical, spiritual, psychological, or any other kind—have purpose and value. Michael White outlined possible purposes and values of this kind of pain as:

> a A testimony to those intentional states [i.e., understandings of self, such as cherished purposes, important values, beliefs and commitments, etc.] held precious by people;
> b A tribute to people's maintenance of a relationship with those intentional states that they continue to revere;
> c A proclamation of people's acts of redress in response to the traumas they have been subject to; and as
> d Expressions that are movements in life that shape opportunities for people to become other than who they were,
> e Elements of a legacy expressed by people who, in the face of the nonresponsiveness of the world around them, remain resolute in their determination that the

> trauma that they and others have gone through will not be for nothing.[36]

Michael White describes these purposes and values as understandings that allow for therapeutic conversations that support the construction of a "robust" sense of self. That is, they lead to conversations about resilience, strength, and overcoming difficulty in relation to trauma.

I think of these understandings of pain as constructive understandings because they help a person to build or rebuild their preferred story in relation to their traumatic experience. These constructive understandings offer rich possibilities to explore during the core trauma work.

To summarize, this pain or anguish can have purposes and values that are specific to each individual. Absent but implicit inquiry allows for the uncovering of these purposes and values.

Distinctions Between Earlier Re-authoring Conversations and Those of the Core Trauma Work

The earlier re-authoring conversations and the later re-authoring conversations of the core trauma work are similar in terms of intent and purpose. Both of these types of therapeutic conversations seek to uncover that which is precious and dear to the individual. They seek to make more accessible and visible these cherished aspects of oneself and thereby strive to make explicit

36 White, M. (2005, September 21). *Michael White workshop notes: Attending to the consequences of trauma*. Dulwich Centre Publications. p. 22. https://dulwichcentre.com.au/wp-content/uploads/2014/01/michael-white-workshop-notes.pdf

that which is absent but implicit. In so doing, both conversations are guided by the concept of the absent but implicit in exploring the preferred story.

That said, I have found that certain types of re-authoring conversations felt safer and easier than others, and I have drawn some conclusions about this. The earlier work of re-authoring (described in Chapter 4) references the effects of the trauma experience and how the individual has stood up to these effects since the trauma experience took place. This work can also draw on the individual's historical material, often a rich source of examples about standing up to the effects of problems that predate the traumatic experience. The key piece is that all of the commitments and cherished values that the individual identifies during this type of conversation are *distanced* in time from the actual occurrence of the trauma experience.

Because this re-authoring work is temporally distanced from the traumatic experience, it involves less intense, emotionally laden material, which makes it safer and easier to navigate. I view these conversations as serving the purpose of creating alternative, preferred associations and meanings that are *indirectly* associated with the traumatic experience.

From a safe distance, these re-authoring conversations allow for the rich development of the individual's preferred story regarding the hardship experience. And the richer the story, the stronger the story. In turn, the stronger the story, the greater the person's sense of personal agency and the greater their sense of safety. In this way, the individual is able to build a secure platform for the re-authoring conversations of the core trauma work that are to follow.

In contrast to these earlier re-authoring conversations, the re-authoring conversations of the core trauma work focus more directly on the individual's *response* to the trauma experience at the time of occurrence. These conversations reference material that is close in time to the trauma experience, and any alternative, preferred associations and meanings created are *directly* associated with the experience.

I believe the immediacy of this connection leads to a greater intensity of emotion associated with the material and thus a greater potential for the individual to become emotionally overwhelmed. The elevated intensity of emotion brings with it an accompanying physiological component—an added complexity that makes navigating this material more challenging. Consequently, I see this type of re-authoring work as higher risk, and because of this, it requires extra safety precautions to be in place in order to navigate it effectively.

To summarize, the key distinctions are:

- Re-authoring conversations that lead up to the core trauma work reference the *effects* of trauma *distanced* in time from the occurrence of the traumatic experience.
- Re-authoring conversations of the core trauma work, which rely more heavily on absent but implicit types of inquiry, reference the individual's *response* to trauma *close* in time with respect to the occurrence of the traumatic experience.

This distinction has implications for the levels of safety or risk. Recognizing when I am entering into the safer re-authoring work versus that of the riskier core trauma work helps me keep a close eye on the level of safety. In other words, being very clear about when I am embarking on the different types of therapeutic conversations helps me to better scaffold the safety piece.

THE CENTRALITY OF THE PHYSIOLOGICAL RESPONSE IN CREATING A SAFE THERAPEUTIC PROCESS

My personal experience with a hardship experience led me to see the body's response to trauma as a more central consideration in the therapeutic process than I had previously imagined. I was convinced that the physiological response to trauma is so powerful and distressing that it must be the focus of the therapeutic process. I came to the conclusion that, in terms of creating adequate safety, the body must lead the therapeutic process. Initially, the mind (or cognitive aspect) takes a back seat.

Once the individual feels confident about sustaining their own safety, it then makes sense for the mind to take a more active leading role in the therapeutic process. In other words, as safety becomes less of a concern, the mind and body can form a more balanced partnership in working through issues related to the trauma experience.

I also came to see the intense physiological response to trauma as being the highest level of alarm that the body can muster. This alarm system is activated by a kind of emotional energy often experienced as psychological pain such as anguish, panic, or overwhelm. It looks and feels very similar to the fight-or-flight response that is triggered when an individual faces a life-threatening situation. This type of response can occur even if, as in my case, the traumatic event is not life-threatening.

In applying this idea to Narrative Practice, I view this powerful physiological response as the body's way of communicating that something very precious and dear to the individual has been violated and negated, resulting in a loss of identity and connectedness. Retrieving and maintaining sufficient safety for the body allows the individual to open up space for the absent but implicit work and provides the scaffolding necessary to recover that which was seemingly lost.

I believe the enormity of the trauma experience explains why individuals with whom I have worked often prefer to use the expression "heart work" to describe the process of healing from a traumatic experience. Language that speaks of the heart carries with it a sense of the human experience that is bigger and deeper than other kinds of descriptions. Understanding the trauma response from this vantage point underscores even more the relevance of the safety piece for individuals as they do the healing work of navigating the territory of violated core truths.

To summarize, I see the intensity of the pain and anguish response as a signal that a traumatic experience has occurred. That signal then tells the body to initiate its most protective mechanism. In other words, the person's alarm system is on high alert because their vital aspects of self have been violated. In this way, the body has taken the lead in protesting the violation.

Because the body's highest level of alarm has been engaged, it will take more than just flipping a switch to disarm the system. It makes sense to me that if it could be easily disarmed, the system would not be robust enough to offer adequate protection. I believe this is why doing only the cognitive work of transforming the meaning of the person's traumatic experience is often not enough to disarm or reset the alarm system.

To carry the alarm metaphor further, there could be several switches that the individual needs to adjust in order to disarm the alarm system following a traumatic experience. Or perhaps an individual wants to do a major overhaul of their alarm system or completely dismantle and rebuild it. Alternatively, the person may just need to recalibrate it. Whatever this work entails, it will be as unique to each individual as is their particular experience of trauma.

I have found that individuals are better served if they work closely with the physiological components of this protective system. That is, it is more effective if individuals work with their bodies, not just their minds, to demonstrate that they are safe and that the most vital aspects of themselves are protected and secure.

To accomplish this, the meaning-making work one does in talking therapy, which relies so heavily on cognitive function (thinking), needs to be integrated with the body. The cognitive meanings of trauma and the embodied meanings of trauma need to be transformed and integrated together. I strive to facilitate this by making the safety of the body a priority.

SCAFFOLDING TASKS FOR A SAFE DEVELOPMENTAL PROGRESSION

My personal experience also highlighted for me that maintaining a sense of safety was connected to navigating therapeutic tasks in such a way that the individual can be in charge of their own process. Or in other words, manageable tasks are safe tasks. For me, this means ensuring that the therapeutic tasks I am offering are a good fit for the individual.

The task is a good fit if the person can navigate it with a sense of personal agency and a bodily sense of safety. Identifying a developmental progression of tasks allows me to better scaffold this good fit. That is, I found that following a developmental progression of tasks—from safer and less complex to riskier and more complex—supports a person to sustain a sense of mastery and safety as they move through the therapeutic process.

In essence, I am applying Vygotsky's ideas about cognitive development and learning[37] to the kind of complex learning that occurs during trauma work. In trauma work, the learning involves more than just cognition. It also has an emotional component that is intimately connected to a physiological component.

I see the safe navigation of trauma work as having a developmental progression that accounts for the cognitive, emotional, and physiological aspects of learning. By identifying and following a developmental progression of tasks, I am striving to work within the individual's zone of proximal development, scaffolding their experience as they navigate the complex learning that is trauma work.

The practices that I have already described (Chapters 1–4) form a developmental progression of therapeutic tasks that set up the safe structure for the absent but implicit inquiry that occurs during the core trauma work. To reiterate:

1. First is the establishment of a therapeutic alliance that is de-centred but influential (Chapter 1).

37 Vygotsky, L. S. (1978). *Mind in society: The development of higher psychological processes* (M. Cole, V. John-Steiner, S. Scribner & E. Souberman, Eds.). Harvard University Press.

2. Next is the acquisition of safety tools such as the breath work, check-ins, and addressing therapy worries (Chapters 2 and 3).
3. Third are the externalizing and re-authoring conversations about the effects of the traumatic response, which are distanced in time from the experience of trauma (Chapter 4).

With careful scaffolding, each of these therapeutic steps is designed to allow the individual to more confidently move to riskier (i.e., more emotionally laden) therapeutic tasks. Any indication of a decrease in a sense of safety, such as increased agitation, signals that the work is moving too fast. It is a sign for the individual to step back to earlier, easier, and safer tasks and shift the work to shoring up the structure of safety.

For instance, my personal experience in the workshop and with CST highlighted the usefulness of a developmental progression of therapeutic tasks pertinent to the absent but implicit inquiry stage of the core trauma work. In particular, I learned that certain work had to be completed first in order to create enough safety that a direct re-telling or the letting-go/holding-on conflict could be safely approached and navigated.

That is, initially, I discovered that even the thought of an indirect re-telling (a story of overcoming a different past hardship) was too overwhelming for me. For me, it evoked the story of the event itself, along with disturbing visual images and a panic response. Consequently, at that moment in time, I did not want to do any type of re-telling, direct or otherwise.

This highlighted for me the risks inherent in a re-telling. Early on in the therapeutic process, this kind of overwhelming response can feed the story of victimization and quickly dismantle the person's sense of safety. However, later on in the process of recovery—namely after working through the absent but implicit pieces—I also found the converse to be true.

My personal experience with the inner conflict of wanting to simultaneously let go of and hold on to the distressing parts of the trauma response further reinforced for me the importance of attending to the progression of the work. In the early stages of healing work, the idea of letting go of any parts of the trauma response can be an overwhelming and unwelcome expectation, as it was for me at the onset of CST. Similar to a premature direct re-telling, the expectation to let go of distress can lead to an individual experiencing inner conflict, confusion, and panic, which in turn also ends up feeding the story of victimization.

However, also similar to a direct re-telling, the converse is also possible. If the individual has first done the untangling work, this letting-go/holding-on conflict can be resolved in a way that thickens their preferred identity story. Indeed, this is one of the main objectives of the absent but implicit inquiry of the core trauma work.

SAFETY PRACTICES FOR THE CORE TRAUMA WORK

Sustaining a bodily sense of safety is important throughout all stages of trauma work, but I see it as most critical during the absent but implicit inquiry of the core trauma work. In order to bolster a bodily sense of safety during this absent but implicit work, I employ all of the body-mind safety tools and the check-in practices described previously. Though I find these practices useful in the earlier work, I consider them essential for the core trauma work.

During the core trauma work is when I make the most use of the breath work techniques, particularly the constructive breath work. The absent but implicit inquiry of the core trauma work is constructive breath work's raison d'être. To reiterate, the main safety practices targeted at managing a bodily (physiological) sense of safety are restorative and constructive breath work, safety check-ins, and body scans.

The practices primarily responsible for creating a safe developmental progression of therapeutic tasks are the narrative practices described previously: the de-centred but influential relationship and the earlier externalizing and re-authoring practices. However, specific to the absent but implicit inquiry of the core trauma work, I have found that two practices in particular support a safe progression of tasks:

1. Introducing an alternative conceptual framework for a person's response to trauma and
2. Checking in with the letting-go/holding-on conflict.

These practices are closely connected, and one often emerges from the other. Usually, I begin by offering the alternative conceptual framework, but on occasion it has made sense to work with the inner conflict first. The order of the tasks depends on the individual's sense of safety.

The conceptual framework I offer to introduce the absent but implicit inquiry rests heavily on the ideas of Michael White described earlier. That is, I present the idea that a person's response to hardship or trauma—pain and anguish—can be seen as an expression that something very precious and dear to them has been violated or subjugated by that experience. (See Chapter 6 for practice examples.)

The second practice of checking in with the letting-go/holding-on conflict means I offer a description of this potential conflict and query if it is relevant to the individual. For example, I ask the person questions like these:

> *Are you experiencing what strikes you as an inexplicable desire to hold on to the pain and anguish of the traumatic experience?*
>
> *I would like to do a check-in with you about something. At some level, does it just feel wrong for you to want to get rid of the hurt and pain associated with this incident/abuse/hardship?*
>
> *Do you feel like you want to hold on tight to the pain and anguish?*
>
> *Do you feel like you should want to get rid of or let go of the hurt and pain associated with the hardship but part of you doesn't want that?*

If this conflict is something the individual is indeed experiencing, I would connect this conflict back to the alternative conceptual framework. That is, I would offer the idea that the person's anguish or pain as a response to trauma can be a sign that something vital to them or something they deeply cherish has been violated.

I would also offer the idea that these cherished aspects are all tangled up with the pain and anguish of the trauma incident, and this entanglement makes it difficult to consider letting go of any of this pain. I then offer the possibility that part of our work together can be about the untangling of these aspects; we can explore the idea of separating the *passion* of cherished values from the *anguish* of the painful experience.

Another way of responding to this conflict is by offering the idea of transforming the intensity of the pain into an intense desire to stand up for what is precious and dear. In other words, I tend to use language that describes transforming the emotional energy of the traumatic experience rather than language that describes letting go of, releasing, or reducing it.

However, I am not suggesting that there is never a time for including the language of letting go, releasing, or reducing. Rather, I see its use as a potential pitfall in the early going. I see the idea of transforming emotional energy as much less threatening than discarding it because the person's desire to protect what is precious and dear may still be entangled with the anguish of the traumatic experience. And though this distinction may shift in later stages of the work, I find initially it is often a very useful distinction for aiding in the untangling of the horror (pain and anguish) from the cherished values that were violated by the experience.

Individuals often respond to this conversation by feeling more settled and safer. As well, by addressing this conflict, we have introduced the idea of an alternative conceptualization of the trauma response. This sets the stage for answering the key absent but implicit question: What precious and dear aspects of you were violated by this experience?

SUMMARY OF KEY PRACTICES

With respect to the absent but implicit inquiry of the core trauma work:

1. Ensure the prerequisite safety work has been completed: the development of a solid de-centred but influential relationship, the acquisition of safety tools, the navigation of therapy worries, and the construction of externalizing and re-authoring conversations that focus on effects distanced in time.
2. Establish the idea that direct re-tellings are optional but *not* required.
3. Introduce the absent but implicit inquiry of the core trauma work by providing the conceptualization that possible responses to trauma have purpose and value.
4. In the early going, offer a check-in practice that describes the letting-go/holding-on conflict.
5. In the early going, offer the idea of transforming the pain and anguish into the passion of reclaiming or standing up for cherished aspects of life if the letting-go/holding-on conflict is pertinent.
6. Maintain a steady focus on safety by utilizing the breath work practices, especially constructive breath work.
7. Remain vigilant about safety, especially if there is a direct re-telling, and be ready to shift to safer ground (i.e., breath work strategies, earlier re-authoring conversations, or a combination of both).

Concluding Thoughts

The concept of the absent but implicit is the guiding principle for the re-authoring conversations that most directly address the pain and anguish of the individual's response to trauma. This is why I call this kind of absent but implicit work the core trauma work. It is here that the person seeks to uncover and reclaim their most precious commitments of life. Doing this kind of therapy can be intense, and it can be very frightening if certain provisions are not in place.

My personal experience gave me a profound sense of appreciation for the importance of safety when recovering from the effects of a hardship experience. Accompanying this appreciation was the recognition of the central role that the body plays in determining safety.

As a result of these understandings, my work shifted to incorporate a myriad of safety practices. To my immense gratification, these practices were welcomed by the individuals with whom I worked. And in the case of Julia, Grace, and Cory, these practices were met with considerable enthusiasm and excitement. It is this enthusiasm that has been the impetus for me to create practices specific to helping individuals more safely navigate the process of healing from hardship.

In the following chapter, I illustrate these practices of the core trauma work in the conclusion of the stories of these three exceptional individuals.

CHAPTER 6

Restoring the Hearth and Returning Home: Core Trauma Work

Julia's Work

Julia declined my suggestion of continuing with the re-authoring work of the previous session (described in Chapter 4).Though it was only our second meeting, she chose to dive right into the deeper, more intense core trauma work.

ESTABLISHING THE ALTERNATIVE PERSPECTIVE

Some individuals approach this part of the work in a slow and tentative manner. Not so for Julia. Her resourcefulness and keen desire to engage in the therapeutic process, which enabled her to cover so much ground in our first session, ushered Julia quickly into the core trauma work in our second session. In response, I offered her the following conceptual framework as a scaffold:

> *You and I have talked about the ways that you have stood up to the effects of abuse, particularly those associated with the Black Tar. I'd like to share with you some more ideas about standing up to the abuse. In particular, I want to share some ideas about how a person's immediate response to the abuse experience can be seen as a form of protest against the*

abuse or a means of standing up to it. The terror or pain or emotional shutdown, for example, can be a way of saying no to it. Perhaps, it's more accurate to say it is a way of shouting "No!" to the abuse.

From this perspective, the pain and anguish act as a strong form of protest. The idea is that if a person were okay with what was going on, they wouldn't have a reaction of pain or fear or anguish or shutdown. And if a person were okay with what was going on, then they might respond with ease and contentment or even indifference. So, the fact that a person responds to a traumatic experience in a certain way—be that with anguish or emotional shutdown or any other similarly notable response—means something.

Carrying this idea further, these kinds of intense responses to the abuse experience are a way of standing up for oneself. The magnitude of the protest points to the fact that one is standing up for something that is very precious and vitally important. In other words, the response to the abuse experience is a sign that something vitally important to the person has been threatened or violated. Does this make sense to you?

Acts of Protest

My intention with presenting this concept was to scaffold the absent but implicit inquiry of the core trauma work. By offering the idea that an individual's response can be thought of as a form of protest, I hoped to create a safe entry point into a conversation with Julia about those vital commitments and values that were violated by the abuse. Instead, Julia used it as an entry point into a conversation about her acts of protest. She did this by jumping into a direct re-telling of what she described as the most significant and horrific sexual attack of her childhood.

In this re-telling, she integrated this new act-of-protest framework as she spoke about her traumatic experience. With a sense of awe in her voice, she listed off several of the actions her 8-½-year-old self had done to protest the sexual assault experience. As she continued to uncover the myriad of ways she had stood up against the assault, Julia marvelled at her childhood self's cleverness and tenacity.

Here are some ways that Julia took a stand against the abuse at the time of the incident:

1. Screaming "No!" She recalled still having a voice at that time, and at the beginning of the attack she distinctly remembered screaming "No!"
2. Physically fighting against the perpetrator's abuse by dragging her feet on the floor so hard she had rug burns on her feet
3. Figuring out she had to stop breathing and struggling during the attack to conserve oxygen when the perpetrator was suffocating her

At this point, I asked:

What does this say about that 8-½-year-old girl, that she responded to the attack in this manner?

Julia replied by describing how she now saw her young self as someone who was capable of tremendous acts of bravery. She expressed a sense of wonder at the cleverness of this girl. She also expressed a deep sense of gratitude for her childhood self's courageous acts of protest and self-protection.

In Julia's words:

> *I was able to see how intuitive, resourceful, and clever that little girl was and how resilient she was, how she was able to survive that violent attack.* [This was] *instead of feeling alone, scared, afraid, and ashamed for attracting the perpetrator and helpless to defend myself, and having that suffocating Black Tar feeling return.*

This new rendition of the abuse experience signalled the beginning of a powerful shift for Julia. She moved from a problem story of victimization and violation to one of personal agency and a sense of empowerment.

At the onset of this conversation, I was surprised at Julia's readiness to launch into a direct re-telling. Earlier, Julia had expressed how relieved she was to know that she could refrain from direct re-tellings in our work together. Plus, she had shared a past example when she had been asked to do a direct re-telling and how this experience had been detrimental to her (described in Chapter 3).

Instead of entering into a direct re-telling, I had expected that Julia would begin to explore what was so vitally important to her that was violated by the abuse experience. I thought our conversation was going to head in the direction of uncovering core values, commitments, and cherished aspects of her life.

Such was not the case. Rather, it made much more sense for Julia to first understand and appreciate the acts of protest embedded in her childhood responses before moving on to the underlying core values that were violated by the experience.

After taking the time to acknowledge the courage and resourcefulness of her childhood self, Julia continued with her re-telling of this incident. She vividly recalled feeling the pressure of the perpetrator's hand as he held her throat and an accompanying intense feeling of being suffocated. Julia remembered looking down on herself from the ceiling, and in retrospect, she wondered if she had had a near-death experience.

At this point in the re-telling, Julia suddenly stopped speaking and stared directly at me with a look of astonishment on her face. "That's why the Black Tar!" she exclaimed. "That's where it came from!" Julia had drawn the connection between her young self's physical suffocation experience at the hands of a violent attacker and the feeling of suffocation that attended whenever the Black Tar showed up in her adult life.

This understanding provided another important shift for Julia. The Black Tar's presence in her life made more sense to her now. No longer was the Black Tar just about victimization. Julia had succeeded in forging a meaningful link between the Black Tar and her 8-½-year-old self's brave acts of protest. The discovery of this connection seemed to further punctuate the significance of her acts of protest.

Julia then explored other ways in which her 8-½-year-old self had been brave and strong despite being rendered physically helpless by a powerful perpetrator. She became more and more animated as she listed the ways that her young self had stood up to this abuse at the time and also how she sustained these acts of bravery throughout her childhood and even into her present life.

These were some ways that Julia's 8-½-year-old self stood up to the abuse at the time and continued to do so long afterwards:

- Repressing her feelings as a small child; she now saw this as a smart and protective choice given her home life at that time.
- Becoming silent as a small child; as with the strategy of hiding her feelings, Julia now saw the silencing of her own voice as a smart and protective choice given her home life at the time.
- Hiding and reading as a small child, creating a way to go off and "lick her wounds" (e.g., waiting for her sister to fall asleep at night so she could put the light under a tent of blankets and read); it was a helpful strategy that Julia continued to use in her life.
- Becoming independent and counting on only herself to take care of herself; this sense of self-reliance had continued to serve her to the present day.

UNCOVERING WHAT IS VITAL OR PRECIOUS

At this point, the conversation easily shifted to speaking about the commitments and values that were subjugated by this abuse experience. I posed the following questions geared at uncovering these absent but implicit pieces:

1. What vitally important part of herself was Julia's 8-½-year-old self taking a stand for?
2. What was it that she was defending that was being suffocated by the attack?
3. What important part of her was she protecting with these acts of protest?
4. What aspects of herself that she holds as precious were being violated by the abuse experience?

Julia determined that the most important thing that was in danger of suffocation from the attack was the value that children get to be protected and cared for. She further elaborated that even 8-½-year-old children get to have a voice. They get to be safe, and they get to be noticed by their moms.

Julia described this particular segment of her work as a major turning point for her. I, too, sensed that this was a pivotal moment in our work together. Julia would later describe it as a game-changer.

LOITERING WITH INTENT: THICKENING THE PREFERRED STORY

Julia used the remaining eight sessions to consolidate and further develop her new perspective and understandings regarding the traumatic childhood experiences through which she had lived. She accomplished this work in several ways:

1. By exploring how this new perspective had led to new meaningful connections and understandings about her traumatic experience:

- Realizing that she had experienced a "turning point" in her healing journey. Julia described the work we did as a kind of "reset" that provided her with an alternative internal structure for understanding her experience of the traumatic incident(s): "I have power over it. It does not have the power over me. The tables have been turned."
- Realizing the importance of not completely forgetting the Black Tar because the pain associated with it served as a reminder that she can do hard work and be responsible for her life
- Realizing how important empathy was to her, which she saw as a positive outcome of the Black Tar. Julia explained, "It has built empathy in me for people struggling with depression and anxiety, and this is really important to me, not to dismiss others' pain and struggle."
- Realizing that, in response to her experience, she had developed excellent empathy skills such as the ability to be open and present, to forgive, and to be able to discern if others are hurting—what she called her "brokenness radar"
- Realizing that the experience of the assailant physically strangling (suffocating) her was connected to the recurring feeling of suffocation she had experienced frequently throughout her life
- Making a second parallel connection that certain recurring bouts of bodily pain were showing up on the anniversary of the abuse and were linked to this experience

2 By naming and elaborating on several positive initiatives she had taken and developments she had fostered since the turning-point work, including:

- Implementing what she had named "the U-turn Method" where she was able to handle the effects of the abuse as they arose in her life. When her mind went to the place of pain, Julia was now able to envision the clever, resilient girl that she had been, and this would prompt her to "stop on a dime and do a U-turn" away from the pain, the sadness, and the loneliness.
- Managing the pain associated with the past abuse in a variety of ways, such as what Julia called "compassionate dissociation," which she defined as compartmentalizing the pain, ignoring it, or just not allowing her mind to spend so much time in the painful place. As Julia explained, "My mind can go there [to the painful memories], and I can now bookend the pain."
- Experiencing a new feeling of acceptance about what happened accompanied by a different level of peace. For Julia, it was a peace associated with not allowing herself to "wallow in self-flagellation: Why me? Why did it happen? Why can't I let it go?, [questions that previously led to] becoming sad and lonely, zoned out, and that [became] a normal way of living."
- Letting go of the past—the Black Tar in particular. Since the turning-point session, the Black Tar and the feeling of suffocation had not visited her. Only a few months prior, the Black Tar had been very debilitating. In addition to the emotional distress it had brought her,

it also had interfered with Julia's ability to care for her children and manage the household responsibilities (e.g., cooking and grocery shopping).

- Resolving trauma-related physical pain and discomfort quickly and easily by using the breath work technique along with intentional thought (a reference to the suffocation feelings and the recurring bodily pain noted above)
- Allowing herself the time and space to make positive changes for herself (i.e., allowing herself to "go off and lick her wounds")
- Creating a wellness team for herself to help her recover from recent and past physical injuries
- Initiating family counselling
- Hosting a safe and welcoming graduation celebration for her children at her home that was a great success
- Sleeping better
- Engaging in less "wallowing" in anxiety and despair
- Acquiring an outward appearance of peacefulness as observed by those around her
- Resisting feeling provoked by difficult situations
- Creating new, positive connections with her children
- Trusting more in her children's abilities and allowing them to be more independent in facing their own challenges
- Communicating better with her husband and finding her voice in a way that she could convey her opinions and wishes in a clearer, calmer manner
- Standing up for her daughter, a high-performance athlete, by challenging unfair coaching practices

- Volunteering to play piano, which was a joyful activity for her, at the local high school
- Hiring a Juno-award-winning piano teacher from whom she was now taking lessons. This was the first thing she had done purely for herself since she moved to her community five years ago.

3 By connecting the expression of her cherished values and commitments—everyone gets to have a voice and children get to be cared for—across time. Julia traced her personal narrative of her cherished commitments by identifying the significant past, current, and future initiatives she had taken, was taking, and intended to take:

- Supporting her younger sister throughout her life to stand up for herself, have a voice, and pursue her life's goals
- Providing ongoing compassion and supportive advice to several members of her extended family
- Acknowledging that she had frequently demonstrated her gift for making space for others' voices and helping them to feel safe, a gift that extended well beyond family members
- Articulating and planning ways she could continue to work on both her immediate and extended family relationships
- Setting the intention to focus on finding new ways to support herself and others in having a strong voice
- Identifying ideas about how to care for her children in a way that supported their growing independence

- Articulating her keen desire to turn her caring focus more on herself by creating a life that went beyond her cherished roles of wife and mother

4 By exploring these original commitments—of having a voice and the caring for and the protecting of children—across her life. Julia was able to identify and lay claim to a whole host of related values, desires, and commitments, thus enriching and enlivening her preferred story. For example, she spoke of the importance of:

- Creating healthy relationships with both immediate and extended family members,
- Supporting young adults in gaining confidence to go after their dreams,
- Having empathy with anyone in her social circle who was struggling with mental health issues, and
- Being independent and able to count on herself.

INCORPORATING THE BREATH WORK

Julia's use of the breath work during the core trauma work paralleled her use of the breath work with the earlier externalizing and re-authoring conversations. She used it in a preemptive manner to address therapy worries, and she also used it to punctuate and deepen newly constructed understandings.

In this context, these understandings were connected to her response to the abuse. As with previous therapeutic conversations, once Julia had articulated an idea that she considered especially important to her, she would ask to incorporate breath work with a statement (or series of statements) that captured the essence of her idea.

The main difference in how Julia applied the breath work in the context of the core trauma work as compared to previous work was the degree to which she used it. She employed the breath work strategies more frequently during this absent but implicit inquiry work than she did with earlier conversations.

The practice of beginning each session with calming and grounding breath work became a consistent pattern for Julia. Julia would use constructive breath work to address therapy worries at the beginning of each meeting.

On one particular occasion, Julia spent several minutes crafting some grounding statements to address her current fears, worries, and concerns about her healing process. She did this by using previous change process statements and customizing them to better match her current thoughts and feelings:

> *I can continue to do work at a pace that is comfortable for me. <breath>*
>
> *I don't have to do all the work of healing from the past abuse all in one go. <breath>*
>
> *I have learned ways to manage the fears and worries associated with the Black Tar, and I can do it now as I continue the work of healing from the past abuse. <breath>*

During the core trauma work, Julia also used the breath work to punctuate and deepen her appreciation of the acts of protest demonstrated by her young self in the face of the assault. Some examples are:

> *I am so grateful for my 8-½-year-old self for doing the very best that she could to fight against the assault. <breath>*
>
> *I recognize the tremendous bravery and resourcefulness of my 8-½-year-old self. <breath>*
>
> *I appreciate the intuition and cleverness of my 8-½-year-old self, and I bring those qualities to the forefront for myself now as I move forwards with this work. <breath>*

One of the most potent times to use the breath work is at that point during the core trauma work when the individual is in the process of transforming the energy of the pain and anguish into the energy of standing up for what is precious and dear. It is this type of intentional transformational work that I had in mind when I first sought to develop the breath work technique.

Following are examples of a few of these types of statements Julia created to do this kind of breath work:

> *I appreciate that the holding on of such pain and anguish has been a way of protecting what is so precious to me, and I am grateful for that part of me for working so hard to keep me safe. <breath>*
>
> *I understand that the enormity of the pain and anguish is a reflection of the importance of that part of me that it represents. <breath>*

I see the pain and anguish as having acted as a kind of personal alarm system for protecting those parts of me that are so vital. <breath>

I no longer need to hold on to the pain in such an intense way. Though it served me once, it no longer serves me to hold on in this way. <breath>

I can let my 8-½-year-old self know that it is okay to turn down the intensity level on my internal alarm system regarding keeping me safe. <breath>

I can work with the 8-½-year-old part of myself to recalibrate my internal alarm system to have a range of responses, so it can activate many different levels of alarm rather than just activating high levels of alarm. <breath>

I can let my 8-½-year-old self know that I have lots of evidence of the ways that my 56-year-old self is excellent at keeping me safe from harm. <breath>

I can let that part of myself that holds on to the 8-½-year-old fear and pain from the assault know that I am now safe from that kind of harm. <breath>

I can let my 8-½-year-old self know that I have developed lots of ways to stand up for what is precious and dear to me—especially the precious value that children get to be loved, protected, noticed, and heard. <breath>

I can let the 8-½-year-old part of myself know that it is now safe to transform the energy of the pain and anguish into the energy of standing up for others. <breath>

This kind of breath work is facilitating the re-authoring of the traumatic experience. This is big work. Safety becomes more of a focus since we are dealing with the core trauma material, which comes with an increased vulnerability to re-traumatization. Consequently, at times, the work becomes less de-centred in order to maintain safety for the individual. It is a context where, as the practitioner, I lean more into the role of keeper of the safety.

This means that I am intentionally guiding the construction of the breath work statements by offering suggestions. These suggestions are based on what the individual has said during our current re-authoring conversation as well as information gathered from previous conversations. Though I am making suggestions for the statements, I am using the individual's ideas and language as much as possible. As well, the expectation that the individual can edit or reject any suggestions remains a guiding principle.

I am also monitoring the individual's level of agitation or excitation and checking in with them to ensure that they are feeling safe and grounded despite the growing emotional intensity of the work. If the individual indicates they are starting to feel too keyed up or overwhelmed, then we would step back to safer territory. There are four main options for accomplishing this:

1 Shift back into the safer re-authoring work, which focuses on effects of the hardship distanced in time. For Julia, that could've been further exploring the effects of the Black Tar and all the ways that she had stood up to the effects

while remaining firmly committed to her values. She had already navigated these types of conversations with more confidence and ease (and sense of safety).

2. Repeat the change process breath work, customizing it to reflect the current work by putting to rest any worry thoughts that have emerged and are contributing to the escalation of agitation.
3. Stop our therapeutic conversation and take up the 5-Minute Breathing Task with an aim at restoring a physical sense of calm.
4. Move through a combination of the above.

Julia also used the breath work to further develop her personal narrative about the values of having a voice and being caring and loving. One of the ways she did this was to explore how she could amplify her voice and keep herself feeling safe in relation to her extended family:

> *I am ready to strengthen my voice in the face of adversity, such as when helping members of my family of origin with their distress and supporting my own family with challenges. <breath>*
>
> *I am ready to begin to figure out a better/different way to be supportive of and give advice to my family of origin. <breath>*
>
> *I can learn to make my interactions with members of my family of origin safer and more peaceful where my emotions are balanced, in check, mature, confident, solid, grounded, authentic, insightful, and wise. <breath>*

I am ready to work on developing my wise, insightful self with regards to members of my family of origin and also with regards to my own family. <breath>

I can develop ways to increase the feeling of a gratifying exchange with members of my family of origin. <breath>

SUMMARY OF JULIA'S WORK

- Exploring the acts of protest of her 8-½-year-old self in the face of a brutal sexual attack, which initiated her shift to a place of personal agency in relation to the childhood sexual abuse
- Making the powerful connection between being suffocated physically as a child and the feeling of suffocation accompanying the Black Tar. This connection seemed to put the Black Tar in a different light, which led to a shift in its influence. It no longer showed up in Julia's life.
- Identifying those aspects of herself that are so vital and precious that were violated by the assault: that children get to be loved, protected, and noticed, and that everyone gets to have a voice, even children
- Transforming the energy of the pain and anguish into the energy of standing up for loving, caring for, noticing, and listening to children
- Thickening the preferred story by uncovering a rich tapestry of values, commitments, and beliefs that developed from the original precious values of caring, protecting, and noticing children and allowing them to have a voice

- Thickening the preferred story by connecting these commitments, values, and beliefs across time and by identifying current initiatives and planning future initiatives
- Identifying the worry that accompanies this kind of effort and resolving this through breath work (e.g., by honouring her own pace of change and reminding herself of her proven ability to make changes)
- Applying the breath work practices throughout the entirety of this core trauma work

Grace's Work

Grace chose to approach the core trauma work by first taking time to bolster her overall sense of safety. She did this by spending more time in externalizing and re-authoring conversations, which focused on the effects of the Past Abuse. The primary effects for Grace were Anxiety and Fear. This work focused on putting Anxiety and Fear in their place and exploring ways she could nurture a sense of peace and calm in her family and work life (as described in Chapter 4).

ESTABLISHING AN ALTERNATIVE PERSPECTIVE

Once Grace had achieved a better sense of peace and calm in her day-to-day life, she initiated the core trauma work. In response to Grace's desire to begin this work, I scaffolded the conversation by presenting her with an absent but implicit conceptual framework:

One way of understanding why the effects of trauma can be so impactful and all-encompassing is that they represent that which is so profoundly important to a person. That is, one reason a person has such a strong response to the traumatic event could be because that traumatic event has violated or threatened core values, beliefs, or commitments that are vital to who they are.

For example, one young woman with whom I have worked spoke about the debilitating effects of the sexual abuse she experienced from an older family member when she was a young teenager. She identified that the abuse had violated two central and cherished values: the ability to be in charge of her own body and keep it safe, and her belief in family togetherness. The violation of these two fundamental core values affected many areas of this young woman's life.

With respect to your situation, what was it that is precious and dear to you, was violated by the Past Abuse perpetrated by your cousin?

UNCOVERING WHAT IS VITAL OR PRECIOUS

In response to this scaffold, Grace readily moved into the absent but implicit work of identifying the values and commitments that are precious and dear to her that were violated by the abuse. During this re-authoring conversation, Grace identified two ages that reflect the significant times in her life when her cousin abused her.

The Protection of a Child's Innocence (9-Year-Old Self)

- A child has the right to engage in childhood activities in a carefree way, including playing with a friend, playing soccer, or going to school.
- A child deserves to visit and be with their grandparents in a safe and caring way. The relationship between child and grandparent is precious, and a child gets to enjoy the fun and special things about visiting a grandparent in a safe way (e.g., be happy and excited, enjoy special treats like sweet cereals and white bread).
- A grandchild gets to enjoy being spoiled by things like watching movies.
- A child gets to learn about their sexuality and body in a child-centred way (not in an adult way).

Families Are Loving and Safe (11-Year-Old/Junior-High Self)

- A teenager or a "tweeny" gets to feel safe in their own home, including feeling safe from violence by members of the extended family.
- A teenager deserves to be protected by their parents from violence or harm in the home; keeping all the children safe from violence in the home is a parent's job.
- Children who are struggling with issues deserve to receive help with the difficulty from their parents.
- Families can interact with, compromise on, and honour the choices of one another.

- Families are not only safe from violence from one another but safe enough that there are positive interactions, caring, and closeness among family members.
- Cousins get to have relationships that are supportive and tight knit like friendships.
- Families have a sense of unity that includes being together, feeling relaxed, having fun, and helping each other; everyone looks out for one another.

LOITERING WITH INTENT: THICKENING THE PREFERRED STORY

Grace used the remaining seven sessions to consolidate and further develop her new perspective and understandings regarding the traumatic childhood experiences through which she had lived. She accomplished this work in several ways:

1. By exploring how this new perspective had led to new meaningful connections and understandings about her traumatic experience:

    - Realizing that an important part of her healing from the Past Abuse was grieving the loss of her innocence and that she could take the time to honour this
    - Realizing that part of her response to the Past Abuse was an elevated sense of vigilance that she had developed into excellent skills of observation (e.g., the ability to accurately read children's expressions, behaviours, and body language)

- Realizing that she could invite more peace and harmony into her life *and* still keep her guard up enough to keep herself and her family safe

2 By naming and elaborating on several positive initiatives she had taken and developments she had fostered since the core trauma work session, including:

- Writing a deeply thoughtful and poignant letter to her cousin where she was able to convey an appreciation of his efforts for reconciliation but also stating her position and level of readiness to engage with him. She let him know in a kind but clear manner that she needed time and space right now and was not ready to work directly with him.
- Developing clear and strong boundaries with the wife of her cousin
- Developing a clear and detailed safety plan for herself and her children for those occasions when they met up with her cousin and his family at family gatherings
- Creating safe and loving family contexts with her own children and husband
- Rewiring her body's safety and security system so that she no longer felt intense alarm and agitation whenever she thought about being around her cousin
- Managing Anxiety and Fear on a day-to-day basis such that their impact was now negligible
- Engaging in positive interactions with her cousin (e.g., friendly birthday text messages back and forth)

- Finding a compassionate and caring place in her heart for her cousin that fit for her. She could care about him but not trust him. She was content to keep a safe distance in terms of intimacy, holding him in an outer circle of family connection. This allowed her to fulfill her wish to participate in extended family gatherings in a loving and safe way.
- Being able to sustain a sense of calm even during extended family gatherings where her cousin was present

3 By connecting the expression of her cherished values and commitments—the protection of children's innocence and the idea that families are loving and safe—across time. Grace did this by identifying specific initiatives in her past and present where she was able to uphold these commitments:

- Protecting and advocating for children in her immediate family context
- Protecting and advocating for children in her professional context of the classroom
- Exploring ways that she could continue this work of protection and advocacy by developing a kind of relational safety plan for her children to ensure their safety in potentially risky family gatherings
- Exploring ways to protect and advocate for children in the classroom context such that she could maintain her sense of composure while still being alert and vigilant with respect to the children's emergent safety concerns

INCORPORATING THE BREATH WORK

Grace used the constructive breath work practice during the re-authoring conversations of the core trauma work to facilitate the transformation of her grief response to the abuse into a response of standing up for the protection of children. The following are some of the understandings from these conversations that she wished to further punctuate and strengthen:

> *I am so grateful to my 9-year-old self for showing me how important the value of innocence is. <breath>*
>
> *With respect to standing up for innocence, I can figure out how to let go of the "icky" parts of the grief of losing my innocence while still holding on to the important value of innocence for children. <breath>*
>
> *I want my 9-year-old self to be okay with transforming the grief energy into the standing up for and the protection of the innocence of children. <breath>*
>
> *I am allowing my 9-year-old self to learn that it's okay to transform the grief energy into the energy of standing up for the innocence of children. <breath>*
>
> *I want to reassure my 9-year-old self that just because I'm getting ready to let go of some parts of the grief of losing my innocence, it does* not *mean that I am letting go of the important value of innocence for children. <breath>*

In fact, I commit to my 9-year-old self that I am going to put that grief energy into helping other children hold on to their innocence. <breath>

I am skilled at standing up for the protection of children's innocence. I did it by keeping distance between my kids and my cousin, and I also did it by switching my daughter's school when she was in a negative environment. I can continue to develop this skill. I give this knowledge to myself now. <breath>

I have been protecting the innocence of children for years, both with my own children and my school children. I'm really good at this. <breath>

I am very good at reading people. <breath>

Sometimes I am too good [at reading people], *but I can use this skill to protect the innocence of children. <breath>*

I can learn how to recognize sooner when this skill is leading me to be worked up and learn how to calm myself down. <breath>

I can use the skill of reading people to stand up for the value of children getting to be innocent. <breath>

I am doing a good job of protecting the innocence of my own children and the students in my classroom. <breath>

My body has a strong sense of truth, and I can trust it. <breath>

And I am happy to be an advocate as required for the other children at my school in protecting their innocence. <breath>

Grace also used constructive breath work to facilitate her change process by calming the worries that were emerging during this part of the work:

I give myself time to figure out how to transform the energy of grief into the energy of standing up for the innocence of children. <breath>

This value of the importance of the innocence of children is so big and important to me that it deserves whatever time and energy is needed in order to transform it into something positive. <breath>

My 9-year-old self and I commit to taking steps in working towards transforming grief into the standing up for the innocence of children. <breath>

I know that baby steps lead to big changes. <breath>

And I have the choice to do small or big steps right now. <breath>

Finally, Grace used the constructive breath work to facilitate her work as she developed a safety plan for herself and her family. Part of her safety plan was the creation of a better "family security system":

I am so grateful to my 11-year-old self for showing me how important it is to feel safe in the family. <breath>

Dear 11-year-old self, you no longer need to alert me through my stomach about the safety in the family. I can keep things safe without that. <breath>

My body is ready to figure out a new security system around being safe in the family. <breath>

My body is ready to learn a different way to monitor family safety and uphold this important value. <breath>

I am so grateful to my body for alerting me when family safety issues arise. <breath>

My 11-year-old self and I can work together to help my body learn a new security system for alerting me to family safety issues, one that is less intense. <breath>

My body is ready to learn how to replace that intense emergency response when I see my cousin and his wife with something less intense. <breath>

There are so many examples/times of feeling safe in my family—decorating the Christmas tree, snuggling with my son at bedtime, reading my daughter books, and playing together. I am giving this knowledge, that I know how to create safety, to my 11-year-old self. <breath>

I have really lived the value of creating a safe family environment. <breath>

I can learn how to cultivate the feeling of being calmer and more grounded when I am around my cousin and his wife. <breath>

I am game to work on becoming very skilled at becoming calm and grounded so that when I do see my cousin, I have those skills more available. <breath>

My body can learn to create a family safety security system that is more calm, confident, and in control. <breath>

I can commit to practicing being more calm, confident, in control, and grounded in the face of other kinds of stress. I can do it through report card time, the holidays, and work. <breath>

I know that this practicing and learning to cultivate calm, confidence, and groundedness in other stressful situations will help me if and when I encounter my cousin. <breath>

SUMMARY OF GRACE'S WORK

- Identifying those aspects of herself that are so vital and precious that were violated by the childhood abuse: the innocence of children gets to be protected, families are loving and safe places
- Developing important understandings that facilitated a shift in her relationship to the Past Abuse: the loss of innocence is a grief experience, one that she felt she could now

properly grieve; the acquisition of skills and knowledges as a result of the Past Abuse that she used to stand in her cherished values; and the ability to create peace and harmony in her life while simultaneously maintaining safety

- Transforming the angst of Anxiety and Fear into the passion for standing up for the protection of children's innocence and for the idea that families are loving and safe
- Thickening her preferred story by identifying several recent initiatives she had taken with regard to living out these cherished commitments, including the development of a family safety plan
- Thickening her preferred story by connecting the expression of her cherished values and commitments—the protection of children's innocence and the idea that families are loving and safe—across time
- Applying the breath work across all aspects of the core trauma work

Cory's Work

Cory entered my office as only Cory can. With a half pirouette, he gracefully alighted on the sofa in a cross-legged position. Straight-backed, his head cocked at an angle of curious inquiry with his hands resting lightly on each knee and his gaze clear and directed at me, he raised his eyebrows in a question of "Okay, what next?" This was his second meeting with me, the purpose of which was to help him deal with the distress he was experiencing after witnessing the murder of a man.

Previously, Cory had quickly mastered the breath work technique and easily navigated the externalizing and re-authoring work in relation to the effects of witnessing the murder. As mentioned in Chapter 4, Cory brought with him a skill set of breathing and spiritual practices and a powerful intellect that allowed him to rapidly move through this earlier work. Not surprisingly, he continued this pace of work and confidently stepped into the re-authoring conversations of the core trauma work.

ESTABLISHING THE ALTERNATIVE PERSPECTIVE AND UNCOVERING WHAT IS VITAL OR PRECIOUS

I introduced the core work by asking Cory the central absent but implicit question of "What was it that is precious and dear to you, was violated by witnessing the murder? What precious aspects of yourself, of who you are, were threatened or subjugated by this experience?" This question turned out to be enough of a scaffold for Cory.

He described his response to witnessing the murder as a feeling of being "shaken" or "rattled." The shock of seeing the violent act of a person being stabbed, coupled with watching that person's physical pain and suffering as he died, shook Cory to his very core. He identified two core values that were violated by this experience:

1. All of us deserve unconditional love, and
2. Death is a peaceful and spiritual experience.

Cory explored the nature of these two core commitments, elaborating on the many ways that he expressed these commitments in his life. During this process of re-examining his beliefs around these two commitments, Cory was able to re-align with them in a way that made sense of the traumatic experience.

LOITERING WITH INTENT: THICKENING THE PREFERRED STORY

Cory used the remaining four sessions to consolidate and further develop his new perspective and understandings regarding the traumatic experience of witnessing the murder. He accomplished this:

1. By exploring new meaningful connections and understandings about his traumatic experience:

    - The realization that he could continue to uphold the value of unconditional love for all while accepting that others in the world did not
    - The further development of his beliefs around death as a peaceful and spiritual experience by seeing it as distinct from the reality of human suffering and pain
    - The acceptance of the reality of the existence of human suffering and pain
    - The conclusion that he was "the master of his own life and that he had the power to be happy"

2 By naming and elaborating on several positive initiatives he had taken and developments he had fostered since the core trauma work session, including:

- Experiencing more calm and not being so "panicky" in his day-to-day life
- Experiencing a decrease in anxiety as evidenced by what he described as the absence of "mind spirals of anxiety" that he saw as connected to an increase in his ability to focus on appreciating and counting his blessings
- Noticing more contentment and happiness in his life
- Noticing that his stomach upset had ceased
- Resuming his usual 45-minute meditations
- Noticing the cessation of violent nightmares and intrusive thoughts
- Being able to recount the story of the murder from a calm, serene place. Cory described this as "leaving the emotions with the experience and just keeping the memory."
- Testifying in court (providing a direct re-telling about the murder) from a place of mastery

3 By connecting the expression of his cherished values and commitments—unconditional love for all and death as a spiritual experience—across time. Cory looked at these commitments as they evolved in relation to the significant relationships in his life:

- He identified and described experiences from childhood involving his nanny.
- He identified and described current experiences involving his friends and his family.
- He identified possibilities for future development of these commitments with his close friends and his mother.

INCORPORATING THE BREATH WORK

Cory used the breath work efficiently and effectively during the core trauma work. He used it to strengthen and punctuate his vital commitments, to transform the energy of his response to witnessing the murder into the energy of standing up for his vital commitments, and to honour and bolster his process of change. Following are some of the breath work statements that he created:

> *I give myself permission to recycle a positive life lesson about the human cycle of death. <breath>*
>
> *I choose to cherish and hold on to the belief that death is a spiritual and peaceful release. <breath>*
>
> *I choose to know that feeling "rattled" is a sign of how important my two values are: my value of having unconditional love for one another and my value that death is a peaceful and spiritual experience. <breath>*

I choose to transform the rattled energy into the energy of conviction for my values of unconditional love for one another and that death is a spiritual and peaceful experience. <breath>

I choose to separate the human experience of physical pain and suffering from the spiritual experience of death, of peace. <breath>

I choose to know/believe that though the murder victim endured physical pain and suffering, he was released from this by death. <breath>

I am free to allow the learning I have gained from witnessing the murder to transform my beliefs, making them stronger and more powerful. <breath>

I choose to release the feeling of being rattled from my body, especially from my belly. It no longer serves me. <breath>

I am ready to create more contentment in relation to my beliefs in 1) unconditional love and 2) death as spiritual and peaceful. <breath>

I know I may have setbacks regarding creating more contentment around these beliefs [of unconditional love and death as a peaceful and spiritual experience], *and I give myself permission to take the time and energy to recover from these setbacks. <breath>*

I am ready to honour my own change and learning in relation to this violent death. <breath>

SUMMARY OF CORY'S WORK

- Identifying those aspects of himself that are so vital and precious that were violated by witnessing the murder. This included the idea that all people deserve unconditional love and that death is a beautiful and spiritual experience.
- Developing important understandings that facilitated a shift in his relationship to the experience of witnessing the murder, the central understanding being that he was the master of his own life and happiness despite the existence of evil and suffering in the world
- Recycling the energy of feeling rattled and shaken into the conviction of standing up for the commitment that everyone deserves unconditional love and that death is a spiritual and peaceful experience
- Thickening his preferred story by identifying several recent initiatives he had taken with regard to living out these cherished commitments, including his ability to create peace and contentment in his everyday life
- Thickening his preferred story by connecting the expression of his cherished values and commitments across time by articulating past and future initiatives in the context of significant relationships
- Applying the breath work across all aspects of the core trauma work

Concluding Thoughts

The core trauma work uses the absent but implicit inquiry to unpack the individual's *response* to the trauma experience. That is, the absent but implicit inquiry is the mechanism by which the individual is able to navigate the re-authoring of their trauma response.

The central question that guides the absent but implicit inquiry is "What was it that is vital and precious to you was violated or subjugated by the traumatic experience?" This work is about uncovering those vital aspects of a person's life that were lost or violated by the trauma experience, reclaiming them, and incorporating them into the preferred storyline of their life.

Using this line of inquiry, the core trauma work enables the individual to explore their vital commitments more deeply, to further acknowledge their value, and to stand more strongly in these commitments by transforming the emotional pain associated with them. The core trauma work is also about connecting these cherished values and commitments across time, which thickens the personal narrative. In these ways, the individual renegotiates their relationship to the traumatic experience.

At the conclusion of this work, the individual has re-authored their preferred story in relation to the trauma experience and shifted from a story of pain and victimization to one of mastery and personal agency.

It is because the work associated with the trauma response has the most emotional and physical charge that it is best negotiated in a manner that makes preserving a sense of safety (and personal agency) for the individual a top priority. I believe it is during this work that the individual is most vulnerable to becoming overwhelmed by the pain and anguish associated with the trauma.

Preparation for a safe developmental progression through the core trauma work takes place during the earlier stages of the therapeutic process. This includes the cultivation of a de-centred but influential relationship, and the incorporation of body-mind safety tools, along with externalizing and re-authoring conversations related to the more distanced or indirect effects of trauma.

Navigating a safe developmental progression during the core trauma work means attending to the timing of certain therapeutic challenges specific to trauma, such as the letting-go-versus-holding-on conflict and direct re-tellings, while simultaneously incorporating breath work practices. As well, providing the scaffold of an alternative conceptual framework of the meaning and purpose of a person's response to trauma is another practice that supports safely addressing these therapeutic challenges.

The conceptual framework that I present in order to set up the absent but implicit inquiry of the core trauma work differs from individual to individual depending on their particular context. When possible, I endeavour to tailor this framework in a way that matches each individual's situation.

For example, with Julia, she had experienced multiple sexual assaults as a young child. This led me to choose a framework that could fit with a young child's experience: saying no to the abuse in the only way she could given her age.

In contrast, with Grace, family connection and safety in extended family gatherings were key values for her preteen self. As these themes were similar to another individual with whom I had previously worked, I incorporated this information into the conceptual framework that I offered to Grace.

For Cory, asking him the opening absent but implicit question "What was it that is precious and dear to you, was violated by the experience of witnessing the murder?" was enough of a scaffold for him to be able to launch into the core trauma work.

Michael White's list of purposes and values of the pain associated with the trauma response (see Chapter 5) offers a range of possible conceptual frameworks to choose from, each of which could be aligned with an individual's particular circumstance.

If the therapeutic process has unfolded in a way that has sustained a bodily sense of safety, then the absent but implicit inquiry of the core trauma work can be an opportune time for a re-telling. In this safe therapeutic context, there is the potential for profound healing.

Julia's spontaneous re-telling about her 8-½-year-old self's sexual assault is a vivid example of this. This experience stands in sharp contrast to her previous re-telling experience (described in Chapter 3). In the more recent re-telling, she was able to stand in a place of personal agency, whereas in the much earlier re-telling, she hailed from a place of helplessness and victimization. One re-telling thickened the preferred story and the other thickened the problem story.

After completing the core trauma work, Cory also engaged in a direct re-telling, which appeared to cement his feeling of triumph over the deleterious effects of witnessing the murder. He did this when he was able to testify in court from a place of mastery about the incident. This re-telling reinforced for Cory his preferred story of being able to sustain peace and contentment in the face of suffering and pain.

These examples show that preserving the safety of the individual does not necessarily mean avoiding re-experiencing the trauma, but rather it is about re-experiencing that trauma from a place of personal agency. The re-telling of the trauma then becomes embedded within the individual's new preferred story of personal agency over the trauma experience. The absent but implicit inquiry of the core trauma work, which includes using breath work practices, supports the individual in finding their way to this safe territory of personal agency where a therapeutic re-telling is not only possible but powerfully healing.

While helpful during all stages of the therapeutic journey, the breath work practices are key to the safe navigation of the core trauma work. It is the breath work tool that is most influential in managing the intense emotion and physical excitation that is inherent in the core trauma work. It is the primary safety tool that I rely on to help privilege the body's experience as the individual works to transform their personal story about the traumatic experience.

I have discovered that although most individuals use the breathing practices to address process change worries and to punctuate epiphanies, one of the most important uses of these practices is when the individuals are doing the transformational work of converting the pain and anguish of the traumatic response into the standing up for their vital and most cherished commitments. If the body feels safe, the individual can feel safe. The breath work plays a large role in taking care of this.

The core trauma work defined by the absent but implicit inquiry is big work. There is an intensity and intimacy to it that is absent in other kinds of therapeutic conversations. I believe this is related to the fact that the individuals are working with aspects of themselves that are central to their understanding of who they are. That is, the individuals are not just re-authoring a preferred story; they are restoring the very essence of who they are. Describing trauma work as heart work seems to best capture the enormity of this undertaking.

As a practitioner, viewing trauma work in this light helps me to better appreciate the responsibility entrusted to me by the individual as I support them through a healing process. As the hearth is to the home, so is the heart to the individual. The absent but implicit kinds of inquiry, combined with the breath work and other safety practices, support the individual in finding peace in their heart. And so, the individual returns home to their true self. The sanctuary of their hearth is restored.

HEART KNOWS[38]

The heart whispers as
the ears listen.

The heart moves
along waves of grief.

The heart fires
through transformation.

The heart
knows the way.

---

38 Schroeder, M. (2022). *Gifts of insight*. Friesen Press. p. 112. Reprinted by permission of the publisher.

Afterword

Dear Julia,

I love circles. And I really like letters. This project started with you, and so it feels right to end it by writing to you. We've come full circle, so to speak, yet the learning from my work with you continues. It ripples out (more circles!).

There are so many sparkling moments for me in our work together: when you nailed the illustration of what you were contending with in your life with the description of the Black Tar; when you got so excited about discovering the tenacity and gutsiness of your younger self and realized she had taught you so much about living bravely, and that you still use and will continue to turn to those skills and knowledges; and when you were so amused by my astonishment and excitement about the clever tactics and strategies of protest of your 8-½-year-old self and how that made you see your younger self in a different way.

That particular conversation was so fun—hard work and intense but ending with such joy and lightness and laughter. It's the kind of conversation that I began to expect with you, one that I strive to recreate with others and will continue to do so.

Then there were the creative ways in which you captured so many of your experiences and learnings, which made working with you so gratifying (and easy). Some of my favourites were the U-turn Method, Compassionate Dissociation, and the

Brokenness Radar. And the icing on this cake was your generosity in allowing me to share these ideas with others.

Another thing that really struck me was just how busy and energetic you were with the work. A couple of months would pass between our meetings, and you would show up citing a whole host of new initiatives and developments.

It was astonishing for me. I couldn't write them down fast enough, which made me wish I was a more sophisticated therapist with fancy recording technology so that I could have captured all the golden nuggets you spoke about. Although, Chapters 4 and 6 would have been considerably longer if I had recorded those sessions.

In any case, those sessions really underscored for me that it's the In-Between Bits that are most important in this work; it's the time between therapy sessions when the really important work gets done. For example, I know that since we last met, you have gone on to stand strong and steadfast as a mom, supporting your two adult children during the global pandemic. I also know that you have moved countries yet again and have begun to create a host of new connections.

I am eager to hear more about those recent developments: What young adults are you mentoring in your new hometown? Have you continued your joy of piano? And how is it going with respect to becoming more at ease with your family of origin?

We are united in the idea that the work we have done together could be of value to others who have faced the kind of tremendous hardship that you have faced. I am guessing that you would also agree that if even one or two of the ideas about keeping safe spark a creative idea here or a conversation there for people, that alone would make the whole thing worthwhile. Here's to hoping that some of these ideas get to splash about a bit and create more ripples in others' lives.

Sending you best wishes from the bottom of my heart,

Caroline

Resources

The following resources have sparked my interest and influenced my work. They may be of interest to those seeking to explore the practices described in this book.

NARRATIVE PRACTICE

Denborough, D. (2014). *Re-telling the stories of our lives: Everyday narrative therapy to draw inspiration and transform experience.* W. W. Norton & Company.

Denborough, D. (2008). *Collective narrative practice: Responding to individuals, groups, and communities who have experienced trauma.* Dulwich Centre Publications.

Denborough, D. (Ed.). (2006). *Trauma: Narrative responses to traumatic experiences.* Dulwich Centre Publications.

Epston, D., Freeman, J., & Lebovits, D. (1997). *Playful approaches to serious problems: Narrative therapy with children and their families.* W. W. Norton & Company.

Hamkins, S. (2014). *The art of narrative psychiatry.* Oxford University Press.

Hedke, L., & Winslade, J. (2017). *The crafting of grief: Constructing aesthetic responses to loss* (1st ed.). (R. Neimeyer, Ed.). Routledge, Taylor & Francis Group.

International Journal of Therapy and Community Works. Dulwich Centre Publications.

Jenkins, A. (1990). *Invitations to responsibility: The therapeutic engagement of men who are violent and abusive.* Dulwich Centre Publications.

Morgan, A. (2000). *What is narrative therapy? An easy-to-read introduction.* Dulwich Centre Publications.

White, M. (2011). *Narrative practice: Continuing the conversations.* (D. Denborough, Ed.). W. W. Norton & Company.

White, M. (2007). *Maps of narrative practice.* W. W. Norton & Company.

White, M., & Epston, D. (1990). *Narrative means to therapeutic ends.* Dulwich Centre Publications.

SOLUTION-FOCUSED BRIEF THERAPY

De Jong, P., & Berg, I. K. (1998). *Interviewing for solutions.* Thomson Brooks/Cole Publishing Co.

de Shazer, S. (1985). *Keys to solution in brief therapy.* W. W. Norton & Company.

Durant, M. (1995). *Creative strategies for school problems: Solutions for psychologists and teachers* (1st ed.). W. W. Norton & Company.

Durant, M. (1993). *Residential treatment: A co-operative, competency-based approach to therapy and program design.* W. W. Norton & Company.

Prescott, D. S., Maeschalck, C. L., & Miller, S. D. (Eds.). (2017). *Feedback-informed treatment in clinical practice: Reaching for excellence* (1st ed.). American Psychological Association.

Talmon, M. (1991). *Single session therapy: Maximizing the effect of the first (and often only) therapeutic encounter* (1st ed.). Jossey-Bass.

TRAUMA/HARDSHIP

Briere, J., & Scott, C. (2014). *Principles of trauma therapy: A guide to symptoms, evaluation, and treatment* (2nd ed.). SAGE Publications.

Herman, J. (1997). *Trauma and recovery: The aftermath of violence—From domestic abuse to political terror.* Basic Books.

Johnstone, M. (2006). *Living with a black dog—His name is depression.* Andrews McMeel Publishing.

Linklater, R. (2014). *Decolonizing trauma work: Indigenous stories and strategies.* Fernwood Publishing.

Maté, G. (2010). *In the realm of hungry ghosts: Close encounters with addiction.* North Atlantic Books.

Trieschman, A. E., Whittaker, J. K., & Brendtro, L. K. (1962). *The other 23 hours: Child-care work with emotionally disturbed children in a therapeutic milieu* (1st ed.). Routledge.

van der Kolk, B. A. (2015). *The body keeps the score: Brain, mind, and body in the healing of trauma*. Penguin Books.

BODY-BRAIN-MIND SCIENCES

Bolte Taylor, J. (2013, August 28). *My stroke of insight* [Video]. TED Conferences. https://www.ted.com/talks/jill_bolte_taylor_my_stroke_of_insight

Kabat-Zinn, J. (2013). *Full catastrophe living: Using the wisdom of your body and mind to face stress, pain, and illness*. Bantam Books.

Maté, G. (2004). *When the body says no: The cost of hidden stress*. Vermilion.

Nestor, J. (2020). *Breath: The new science of a lost art*. Riverhead Books.

Porges, S. W. (2011). *The polyvagal theory: Neurophysiological foundations of emotions, attachment, communication, and self-regulation* (1st ed.). W. W. Norton & Company.

Siegel, D. (2012). *Pocket guide to interpersonal neurobiology: An integrative handbook of the mind*. W. W. Norton & Company.

Upledger, J. E., & Vredevoogd, J. D. (1983). *Craniosacral therapy*. Eastland Press.

Weil, A. (1999). *Breathing: The master key to self healing* [Audio CDs]. Sounds True.

MINDFULNESS

Hanh, T. N. (2013). *Body and mind are one: A training in mindfulness* [Audio CD]. Sounds True.

Kabat-Zinn, J. (2005). *Wherever you go, there you are: Mindfulness meditation in everyday life*. Hachette Books.

Kabat-Zinn, J. (2005). *Guided mindfulness meditation series 1* [Audio CD]. Sounds True.

Puddicombe, A. (2012). *All it takes is 10 mindful minutes* [Video]. TED Salon London.https://www.ted.com/talks/andy_puddicombe_all_it_takes_is_10_mindful_minutes

Weil, A., & Kabat-Zinn, J. (2001). *Meditation for optimum health: How to use mindfulness and breathing to heal your body and refresh your mind* [Audio CD]. Sounds True.

www.mindfulschools.org

YOGA[39]

Devi, N. J. (2007). *The secret power of yoga: A woman's guide to the heart and spirit of the yoga sutras.* Harmony.

Iyengar, B. K. S. (2013). *Light on pranayama: The definitive guide to the art of breathing.* HarperCollins.

Rothenberg, R. L. (2019). *Restoring prana: A therapeutic guide to pranayama and healing through the breath for yoga therapists, yoga teachers and healthcare practitioners.* Singing Dragons.

MEANING-MAKING

Cameron, J. (2002). *The artist's way: A spiritual path to higher creativity.* J.P. Tarcher/Putnam.

Frankl, V. E. (2006). *Man's search for meaning.* Beacon Press.

McGoldrick, M., & Gerson, R. (1985). *Genograms in family assessment.* Penguin Books.

Schroeder, M. (2022). *Gifts of insight.* Friesen Press.

Vygotsky, L. S. (1978). *Mind in society: The development of higher psychological processes.* (M. Cole, V. John-Steiner, S. Scribner & E. Souberman, Eds.). Harvard University Press.

39 My understanding of yoga breathing techniques comes from years of attending yoga classes and workshops and not from studying the literature. Michelle Schroeder, yoga teacher and co-founder of Ajna Yoga Studio and Yoga Therapy College, has provided these resources for those interested in exploring breath work and yoga.

APPENDICES

Appendix A: The 5-Minute Breathing Task

PURPOSE: A MINDFULNESS EXERCISE to create calm and focus in the mind and body.

The 5-minute breathing task has three parts: measuring one's initial breathing rate (1 minute), practicing mindful breathing (3 minutes), and measuring one's final breathing rate (1 minute). I developed this task over time, but I drew the main ideas for it from the yoga and mindfulness meditation worlds. As well, this type of breathing task is based on the work of Andrew Weil,[40] and the idea of practicing at least 3 minutes of breathing is based on the work of Julie Brock.[41]

Figure out your current breathing rate by counting how many breaths you take in 1 minute. Most people say it is easiest to count as follows: 1 breath = 1 inhalation + 1 exhalation.

Determine which of the following zones your breathing rate is in:

- **ZONE 1:** The Chill or Relaxed Zone of 1–8 breaths/minute
- **ZONE 2:** Everyday Operational or Medium Zone of 8–15 breaths/minute

40 Weil, A. (1999). *Breathing: The master key to self healing* [Audio CDs]. Sounds True.

41 Brock, J. (n.d.). *Breath work as a relaxation technique for reducing stress in children with a diagnosis of obsessive-compulsive disorder* [Workshop]. Calgary Board of Education, Calgary, Alberta.

- **ZONE 3**: Somewhat Excited/Agitated Zone of 15–22 breaths/minute
- **ZONE 4**: Very Excited or Very Geared-Up Zone of 22+ breaths/minute

Please note: I have created the zones from a variety of sources (e.g., athletic training, individuals with whom I have worked, etc.), and they are merely guidelines.

Decide which zone you would like to achieve. If your preferred zone is *lower* than the one you are currently in, then proceed with the following.

For 3 consecutive minutes, breathe in the following manner:

- Make the in breath half the length of the out breath. These breaths need to be of a decent length, so choose a count of 4 for the inhalation and 8 for the exhalation or 3 for the inhalation and 6 for the exhalation. Count full seconds by saying slowly "One one thousand, two one thousand, three one thousand, etc." in your head as you count.
- Breathe all the way down to your belly button for each breath. That is, on the inhalation, feel your lower belly expand, and on the exhalation, feel your lower belly contract (think of your belly button moving towards the back of the spine). Sometimes it helps to direct the breath by putting one hand on your belly and the other on your chest so that you can monitor how you are breathing. Ensure that you are *not* breathing with your upper chest only.
- If you feel light-headed, it likely means that you are not breathing deeply (i.e., you are not belly breathing); instead, you are shallow breathing (just with your upper chest), or

you may be breathing too fast. Pause and breathe normally for a few minutes, then try again.

After 3 minutes of doing this breathing technique, check your breathing rate again. The hope is that you have moved yourself to the lower zone. Sometimes, it may take repeating the technique in order to create the desired impact of a slower breathing rate and a calmer mind. As long as the task is not escalating your breathing rate, it makes sense to repeat the task again.

However, if doing this breathing exercise is creating the opposite response—that is, if it is making you feel more stressed and keyed up—then stop. Take a break and do other activities that you know to be calming for you. Then, if you want to attempt the exercise again, do so with the support of a knowledgeable helper.

After you have completed at least one cycle of the breathing, take some time to observe and reflect. Notice how your body feels. Notice how your mind feels. What and how is your body feeling? What and how is your mind thinking? What is different?

This technique can be used anytime, anyplace to bring yourself into a calmer and more focused state. If you practice this enough *and* set the intention, you can create a new baseline breathing rate for yourself. That is, if you discover that your usual resting breathing rate is 17 breaths per minute and you want your usual resting (or baseline) breathing rate to be lower, then clearly set the intention of what rate you want.

For example, decide on a number that fits for you right now and say to yourself, "I want my resting breath rate to be 15 breaths per minute." Then, practice the 3-minute exercise. After some practice, you will find that your resting breathing rate has dropped.

As well, with practice you will be able to slow your breathing down almost immediately (i.e., you won't even have to do a full 3-minutes worth of practice). This skill is very useful in stressful situations when you are experiencing feelings of unwanted tension or agitation.

It is important that when you are first learning this type of breathing activity to make sure you do the slow breathing part of the exercise for *at least* 3 minutes. The reason behind this is that if you are all geared up, chances are you have been that way for a while, and somehow, you have been telling your mind and body to be in that state (e.g., by having lots of worry thoughts, trying to do too many things at once, rushing too much, drinking too much caffeine, etc.). In order to switch from a geared-up mode to a more relaxed mode, you need to convince your body that it is okay (and safe) to do so.

Doing 1 or 2 or even 10 relaxed breaths will not be enough to override all the earlier stress (or fear) messages. I have learned that it generally takes a minimum of 15–20 relaxed breaths in a row to convince the body to switch modes. At least, this is likely the case when you are first learning how to do this.

In fact, it may take more than 20 breaths in the early stages; everyone starts at a different place with respect to stress levels. However, 3 minutes allows for the minimum 15–20 breaths, so it is a good starting point. It is helpful to set a timer so you can focus on the quality of your breathing rather than on the counting.

The general idea behind this task is that if you are breathing in a very rapid manner, you are likely quite stressed or overexcited; focus and concentration are likely compromised. Therefore, teaching yourself to be in an optimally relaxed state and how to get into that state will help with focus, concentration, and stress management.

Another idea behind this exercise is that it is a stepping stone towards learning other mindfulness practices. Currently, there is evidence that mindfulness meditation helps reduce stress and improve attention and focus. There has been a lot of excitement in the field of psychology and medicine about the benefits of even a few minutes per day of mindfulness meditation.

Appendix B: Addressing Therapy Worries

THERAPY WORRIES THAT COULD GET IN THE WAY

These are examples of worries, fears, and doubts that can get in the way of doing the work of healing from the effects of trauma and hardship. I have gathered them from individuals with whom I have worked. They are fairly generic and can be offered as possibilities to individuals who are just beginning to do this work. They are more effective if individuals customize them to fit their particular situation.

- A TREMENDOUS SENSE OF IMMEDIACY: "I have to fix everything right away today or soon after today."
- ALL-OR-NOTHING THINKING: "If I don't fix all the concerns associated with this issue, then I am a failure."
- FEAR OF FAILURE AND SETBACKS: "I will fail in my attempts to resolve my problem. I will remain stuck in the same place. Things may even get worse."
- PROBLEM HISTORY LOGIC: "This problem has been around a long time and has been a huge problem for me. Therefore, it must inevitably take a long time to shift it or feel some relief from it."

- **PROBLEM INTENSITY LOGIC:** "Working with trauma and hardship means I have to go into the dark place, the 'pit of despair,' in order to heal from that despair. This kind of work has to be long, relentless, arduous, and despairing work."

PREFERRED COUNTERSTATEMENTS FOR ADDRESSING THERAPY WORRIES

These are examples of preferred counterstatements to worries, fears, and doubts that I have gathered from individuals who have worked with me in the past. These can be offered as possibilities to individuals who are beginning this work, and if relevant, they can be customized for each individual's situation.

To Address a Sense of Immediacy and All-or-Nothing Thinking:

- I can take the time I need to do this work. <breath>
- I don't have to rush. <breath>
- I understand and I am okay with the fact that I don't have to fix everything right away. <breath>
- I can honour my own pace of change. <breath>
- I can be open to figuring out my pace of change and what it will look like. <breath>
- It's okay for me to take some time to learn these calming techniques. I know that doing the breath work and learning to calm/soothe myself is part of my healing process. <breath>
- I can learn how to take the time to figure out what my best pace of work/change is. <breath>

- I am okay with the idea that there is no universal right or wrong way for me to do this work. I can take the time to figure out what is right for me. <breath>
- I am okay with taking small steps, knowing that small steps can lead to big changes. <breath>
- Big epiphanies with regard to my work are welcome and wonderful, but I can acknowledge smaller learnings and know they count and are important with respect to heading in the right direction. <breath>
- I can be open to the idea that my pace of change may vary. Sometimes I will experience significant change, and other times changes might be more modest, but I am open to discovering that. <breath>
- I am open to healing in whatever fashion feels good and right to me. <breath>

To Address the Fear of Failure and Setbacks:

- I am ready to figure out ways to work on fears and anxiety associated with Problem X or Concern Y. <breath>
- I recognize that fears and anxiety about not moving forwards are all part of the learning, and I am up for this learning. <breath>
- I know how to be grounded, centred, calm, and at peace. I am grounded, centred, calm, and at peace when I [insert personal example here], and I can learn how to be this way as I learn to manage fear of failure. <breath>
- I know that this learning might not be steady and that I may encounter setbacks. However, I am ready to find ways to get back on track faster after a setback. <breath>

- Setbacks do not have to be counted as failures. I can see them as signs of more or different learning being required. And I can give myself the time and energy to figure out what that learning might look like. <breath>
- I have experienced setbacks with regard to Problem X or Concern Y before, and I have been able to come back from some of those setbacks. I did it when A, B, C happened. And I know that I can use that knowledge and experience to help myself right now in moving forwards. <breath>
- Experiencing a setback does not mean that I am back to square one. It does not negate the work I have done. It is a part of the process of changing patterns and habits. It provides me with clues about the direction of the work I need to do next. <breath>
- I know, with the help of my loved ones, friends, and family [helpful to name them each individually], I can find my way through to a calm place of healing. <breath>

To Address the Problem History Logic:

- I can be open to the idea that just because a problem has been around for a long time does not mean that it has to take a long time before I can make some significant change with regard to the problem. <breath>
- I can consider the idea that even if the problem has been around a long time, I can find some relief from it in a relatively short time. <breath>
- I can be open to the possibility that I can get some pretty significant relief from this issue in a relatively short time. <breath>

- Even though this problem and its effects have been around a really long time, I am open to the idea that I can take some important steps in reducing the impact of this problem in a relatively short time. <breath>
- Worry thoughts may be persistent, but so am I, and I am committed to being persistent in learning how to put these thoughts in their place as many times as I need to. <breath>

To Address the Problem Intensity Logic (Trauma or Tremendous Hardship Logic):

- I can be open to the idea or the possibility that healing from the effects of trauma/hardship can be releasing and liberating work and that it does not have to be despairing, overwhelming, and frightening work. <breath>
- I can be open to learning ways to keep this work on the side of releasing and hopeful work and away from the despairing, the overwhelming, or the hopeless side of work. <breath>
- I know how to be grounded, centred, calm, and at peace. I have experienced being this way when I [insert a grounding experience here such as doing yoga, nursing their baby, walking in the woods], and I give that knowledge to myself now so I can use it to learn how to manage the fear and anxiety that accompanies this work. <breath>
- I know that the intensity of this problem likely means that this will be hard work. Hard work does not have to be hopeless, despairing, or overwhelming work. Hard work can also be gratifying, fulfilling, and satisfying work. I am ready to figure out how to address Problem X (e.g., the

effects of trauma) with the satisfying kind of hard work. <breath>

- I am not afraid of hard work. I can do hard work. It is hopeless, despairing, and overwhelming work that I do not want to do. I can be open to doing hard work that is on the hopeful, gratifying side of things. <breath>
- I recognize that there is the potential for this work to veer off into despairing, hopeless, and overwhelming territory. However, I am open to figuring out ways of making these forays into the dark places easier and quicker to return from. <breath>
- I have fallen into the despairing, overwhelming, and hopeless place with regard to this issue (e.g., trauma/abuse/hardship) in the past, and I have been able to get out of that place. I acknowledge that I am ready to learn more ways to take myself out of that disturbing place should I find myself back there again. <breath>

Appendix C: Breath Work Sleep Statements

SLEEP STATEMENTS WORK BEST when they specifically address the individual's current worry thoughts—both worry thoughts connected with problems but also worry thoughts connected with the inability to get to sleep:

- It's okay for me to take some time to learn these calming techniques. <breath>
- I know that doing the breath work and learning to calm/soothe myself is part of my healing process. <breath>
- Even if I can't get to sleep right away, I know that doing these relaxing breath work exercises is healing for my body. <breath>
- I know that I need to figure out how to proceed with healing from the trauma/hardship/abuse and that it will be confusing at times. I am committed to working through the confusion in ways that are healthier and better for me. And I can tell my mind and body that this figuring out can happen tomorrow with my partner/friend/whomever or at some other time, not now/at bedtime. <breath>
- I can figure out which work is my work and which work is *not* my work, and I give myself the time and space to figure this out. <breath>

- The time and the space to figure this out is tomorrow, not now/at bedtime. <breath>
- I am a person who can learn to let go of worry thoughts at bedtime. < breath>
- I am a person who is learning how to develop calming bedtime practices. <breath>
- Mind, I am grateful to you for being so vigilant, but now it is time to let go of vigilance and embrace quiet. You can be vigilant tomorrow. <breath>
- I am not afraid of hard work; I am committed to working hard to heal, and that includes learning to let go of worry thoughts at bedtime. <breath>
- Worry thoughts may be persistent, but so am I, and I am committed to being persistent in learning how to put these thoughts in their place. <breath>
- I am free to learn new ways to be in charge of worry/busy thoughts so that they don't get in the way of good sleep. <breath>
- I am committed to creating ways that will help me calm myself and get the healing sleep I want. <breath>

Appendix D: Breath Work Prayer Statements

FOR SOME INDIVIDUALS, faith plays a significant role in how they make meaning in their lives, and prayer is an important aspect of that. This is an example of a way that individuals can use breath work statements of the preferred story to create a prayer that supports them in sustaining the work of healing in their daily life:

- God, help me to let go and change the belief that the way things have been with me and sleep problems is the way things have to stay. <breath>
- God, help me to let go of and transform the idea that it has to be hard/impossible to find ways to improve my sleep patterns. <breath>
- God, help me to release and transform the idea that I have to lose sleep about worries to do with my family/children/the past abuse/hardship. <breath>
- And, God, help me to let go of and change the belief that changing my sleep pattern has to be difficult. <breath>
- Dear God, help me to learn that it's okay for me to take some time to learn these calming techniques. <breath>
- Dear God, help me to embrace the knowledge that doing the breath work and learning to calm and soothe myself is part of my healing process. <breath>

- Dear God, help me to embrace the knowledge that even if I can't get to sleep right away, doing these relaxing breath work exercises is healing for my body. <breath>
- I know that I need to figure out how to proceed with healing from the abuse and that it will be confusing at times. I am committed to working through the confusion in ways that are healthier and better for me. And, with God's help, I can tell my mind and body that this figuring out can happen tomorrow with my partner/friend/whomever or at some other time. I don't have to dwell on it now at bedtime. <breath>
- I know, with God's help and with the help of my loved ones [name them], I can find my way through to a calm place of healing. <breath>
- Dear God, help me figure out which work is my work and which work is *not* my work and give myself the time and space to figure this out. <breath>
- With God's help, I can accept that the time and the space to figure this out is tomorrow, not at bedtime. <breath>
- Dear God, help me to remember that I am a person who can learn to let go of worry thoughts at bedtime. <breath>
- With God's help, I am a person who can use my faith to help me learn how to let go of worry thoughts at bedtime. <breath>
- With God's help, I know I am a person who can learn how to develop calming bedtime practices. <breath>
- Dear God, help me to remember all that I am grateful for: my son, [name]; my daughter, [name]; my partner, [name]. <breath> They soothe my soul. <breath>
- Dear God, I am so grateful for my loved ones. <breath>

- Mind, I am grateful to you for being so vigilant, but now it is time to let go of vigilance and embrace quiet. You can be vigilant tomorrow during the day. For tonight, I hand this vigilance over to God's keeping. <breath>
- I pray for the strength to remember that I am not afraid of hard work. I am committed to working hard to heal, and that includes learning to let go of worry thoughts at bedtime. <breath>
- Worry thoughts may be persistent, but so am I. I can use my faith in God to strengthen my commitment to learning how to put these thoughts in their place. <breath>
- My faith in God helps me learn new ways to be in charge of worry thoughts/busy thoughts so that they don't get in the way of good sleep. <breath>
- Dear God, help me to sustain my commitment to creating ways that will help me calm myself and get the healing sleep I want. <breath>

Acknowledgements

Cory, Julia, Grace, and the many other individuals I've worked with, you have gifted me with the privilege of accompanying you on your healing journeys. Your work has provided the inspiration and substance for this book.

Tara Ouellette, Shelley Cervi, Holly Dalgliesh, and Michelle Schroeder, your teachings about body-mind connection have served to elucidate and broaden my understanding about healing.

Jessica Sherer, Jazmin Welch, Lynn Slobogian, and Lisa Maxwell, my publishing and editing team, your skill, commitment, and meticulous care has not only helped bring this book to life but has made the process a rich learning experience for me.

Sophia, Zachary, and Julian, my children, from whom I have learned the lessons about joy, love, hope, and loss that only a child can teach, what you've taught me has supported my work with children, youth, and their caregivers in countless and untold ways.

Kingsley and Patricia Payne, my parents, you have gifted me with the joy of learning and taught me about compassion and kindness. In particular, my father—instructor, academic advisor, and editor—has been a loving and enthusiastic co-pilot on countless narrative flights, including this one.

Lastly, Kevin Wright, my husband, your steadfast patience, constant love, and cheeky humour is the safe harbour to which I always return after the storm (creative or otherwise).

Thank you all from the depths of my heart.

Caroline

Photo credit: Sig Novak

CAROLINE WRIGHT holds a Master of Science in Clinical Psychology from the University of Calgary and works in private practice with children, youth, and their caregivers. She provides therapy through a narrative practice lens that draws upon her experience working in a diverse range of settings. These include a children's developmental clinic, child and youth residential treatment programs, treatment foster care, youth outreach, and specialized school-based programs.

Caroline and her husband live in Victoria, Canada, where they enjoy spending time with their three adult children and two grandchildren.

Manufactured by Amazon.ca
Acheson, AB

12000357R00169